WHY CHILD CARE MATTERS

Preparing Young Children For A More Productive America

A Statement by the Research
and Policy Committee
of the Committee for Economic
Development

⊛CED

Library of Congress Cataloging-in-Publication Data

Why child care matters: preparing young children for a more productive America /a statement by the Research and Policy Committee of the Committee for Economic Development.
  p. cm.
  Includes bibliographical references.
  ISBN 0-87186-096-1 : $14.50
  1. Child care — United States. 2. Child care — Government policy — United States.
3. Child development — United States. 4. Education — Social aspects — United States.
I. Committee for Economic Development. Research and Policy Committee.
HQ778.7.U6W548 1993
649. — dc20   93-15304
                                                               CIP

First printing in bound-book form: 1993
Paperback: $14.50
Printed in the United States of America
Design: Rowe & Ballantine

COMMITTEE FOR ECONOMIC DEVELOPMENT
477 Madison Avenue, New York, N.Y. 10022
(212) 688-2063

2000 L Street, N.W., Washington, D.C. 20006
(202) 296-5860

CONTENTS

WHY CHILD CARE MATTERS

**Preparing Young Children
For A More Productive
America**

RESPONSIBILITY FOR CED STATEMENTS ON NATIONAL POLICY

The Committee for Economic Development is an independent research and educational organization of some 250 business leaders and educators. CED is nonprofit, nonpartisan, and nonpolitical. Its purpose is to propose policies that bring about steady economic growth at high employment and reasonably stable prices, increased productivity and living standards, greater and more equal opportunity for every citizen, and improved quality of life for all.

All CED policy recommendations must have the approval of trustees on the Research and Policy Committee. This committee is directed under the bylaws which emphasize that "all research is to be thoroughly objective in character, and the approach in each instance is to be from the standpoint of the general welfare and not from that of any special political or economic group." The committee is aided by a Research Advisory Board of leading social scientists and by a small permanent professional staff.

The Research and Policy Committee does not attempt to pass judgment on any pending specific legislative proposals; its purpose is to urge careful consideration of the objectives set forth in this statement and of the best means of accomplishing those objectives.

Each statement is preceded by extensive discussions, meetings, and exchange of memoranda. The research is undertaken by a subcommittee, assisted by advisors chosen for their competence in the field under study.

The full Research and Policy Committee participates in the drafting of recommendations. Likewise, the trustees on the drafting subcommittee vote to approve or disapprove a policy statement, and they share with the Research and Policy Committee the privilege of submitting individual comments for publication.

Except for the members of the Research and Policy Committee and the responsible subcommittee, the recommendations presented herein are not necessarily endorsed by other trustees or by the advisors, contributors, staff members, or others associated with CED.

RESEARCH AND POLICY COMMITTEE

*Voted to approve the policy statement but submitted memoranda of comment, reservation, or dissent. See page 68.

X

PROJECT DIRECTOR

SANDRA KESSLER HAMBURG
Vice President & Director of
    Education Studies
CED

PROJECT EDITOR

JULIE WON
Assistant Director of Information
CED

SENIOR PROJECT ADVISORS

DANA E. FRIEDMAN
Co-President
Families and Work Institute

ELLEN GALINSKY
Co-President
Families and Work Institute

PROJECT ASSOCIATES

TERRA GEIGER
Policy Analyst
CED

MICHAEL B. GREENSTONE
Policy Analyst
CED

TAMARA L. ADLER
Research Assistant
CED

PURPOSE OF THIS STATEMENT

As an organization that has long recognized the importance of human resource development to the nation's economic competitiveness, CED believes that our country's response to its child care needs has important implications for both the current and the future productivity of its labor force.

In four previous policy statements, *Investing in Our Children: Business and the Public Schools* (1985), *Children in Need: Investment Strategies for the Educationally Disadvantaged* (1987), *An America That Works: The Life-Cycle Approach to a Competitive Work Force* (1990), and *The Unfinished Agenda: A New Vision for Child Development and Education* (1991), CED developed a broad strategy for strengthening the nation's human resources through improved public and private investment in education, early childhood development, targeted aid for disadvantaged children and youth, and policies to enhance the productivity of workers on the job. Each of these reports recognized the importance of greater investment in children's early development and education to the nation's long-term economic vitality and social strength.

Child care has become a critical part of the "human investment strategy" CED developed in its policy statements on education and work force issues. Both *Children in Need* and *The Unfinished Agenda* called for a comprehensive and coordinated strategy for meeting the developmental needs of children, particularly the disadvantaged.

Why Child Care Matters examines the critical role that child care plays in the way an increasing number of children are growing, learning, and preparing for school and for life. Of course parents have the primary responsibility for their children's care. But as a society, we all benefit when children have high-quality care in their earliest years that will help them succeed in school and later as citizens and workers.

AN IMPORTANT SOURCE

A primary resource for our study has been a CED-sponsored background research paper entitled *Education Before School: Investing in Quality Child Care*. Prepared by Ellen Galinsky and Dana Friedman, copresidents of the Families and Work Institute who also served as senior project advisors, the study provides a wealth of information on the state of child care in the United States. This study has been published for CED by Scholastic Inc.

ACKNOWLEDGMENTS

We believe this report contains both good policy and good common sense. It is also a statement that comes from the deep personal commitment of the CED trustees and the advisors who served on this subcommittee. Key to the success of this project has been the steadfast leadership of Robert E. Campbell, vice chairman of Johnson & Johnson. Bob's humanity, vision, and personal commitment to a better start for all children were this project's driving force.

I would like to draw special attention to the contribution of this study's project director, Sandra Kessler Hamburg, CED's vice president and director of education. Sandy's breadth of knowledge, her experience in children's and education issues, and her ability to bring together disparate perspectives have enriched this project immeasurably.

Special thanks are also due to the important contributions of senior project advisors Ellen Galinsky and Dana Friedman and to the publisher of their study *Education Before School,* Scholastic Inc. Thanks are also due to CED Policy Analyst Terra L. Geiger and Tamara L. Adler, research assistant.

We are also deeply indebted to the exceptional subcommittee of CED trustees and advisors who developed this report's recommendations. They are listed on page x.

In addition, we would like to acknowledge the important financial and intellectual contribution made by the corporate and private foundations, listed on page 69, that have so generously supported this project.

Josh S. Weston
Chairman
CED Research and Policy Committee

Chapter 1

CARING FOR AMERICA'S CHILDREN:
Introduction and Summary of Recommendations

Once of little concern outside the family, the care and early education of young children have now become high priorities for public policy. The convergence of two major economic and social trends has thrust the issues of child care quality, availability, and affordability into the spotlight.* First, an increasing proportion of women have chosen to enter the labor force. This has been both a result and a cause of major cultural, social, and economic changes during the last three decades. This, in turn, has created unprecedented growth in the number of young children needing out-of-home child care in their earliest years. By 1991, 58 percent of mothers with children under age six were in the labor force, a more than threefold increase since 1960.[1] Second, the nation's alarm over the declining academic achievement of its students has focused national attention on how poorly many American children are prepared for school. In recognition of this, the first of the National Education Goals established in 1990 states: "By the year 2000, all children in America will start school ready to learn."

WHY CHILD CARE MATTERS

Increasingly, child care has become an issue in which children, parents, business, and society have a converging interest. Our youngest children need good care to ensure their proper education and development and to prepare them for productive lives. Parents who must work or finish school need to know their children are well cared for. Business and the economy as a whole gain a more productive work force when employees feel confident that their children are secure and learning. And society as a whole benefits when more families are self-sufficient and the next generation of citizens is well prepared for its adult responsibilities.

More American children than ever before are spending their days in out-of-home care. Between 1976 and 1990, the number of child care centers tripled, and the number of children cared for in these programs quadrupled.[2] Of the nation's 22 million children under the age of six in 1990, 12 million lived in families in which either both parents worked or the only parent worked.[3] Approximately 8 million of these children were in some form of out-of-home care: between 4 and 5.1 million in 80,000 centers, about 700,000 in 118,000 regulated family child care homes, and about 3.3 million in an estimated 555,000 to 1.1 million unregulated family child care homes.

DEVELOPING OUR CHILDREN: THE CONNECTION BETWEEN CHILD CARE AND EDUCATION

From the moment they are born, children are learning the critical cognitive, physical, social, and emotional skills they will need for later success both in academics and in life. This underscores the need to focus on the development and education of all children, particularly those who start life disadvantaged by such factors as poverty, racial discrimina-

---

*See memorandum by OWEN B. BUTLER (page 68).

tion, lack of English-language skills, and family and community breakdown. Successful development depends on the quality of a child's early experiences, whether these occur while the child is in the care of a parent or someone else. Poor-quality care can hamper what and how well children learn, their readiness for formal schooling, and their future success in school, at work, and as citizens. **All forms of child care, including parental care, should meet the developmental needs of children.**

HELPING PARENTS WORK

Parents use child care for many reasons. Many parents, whether or not they work, frequently use child care to provide their children with greater educational experiences and opportunities for socialization. Child care may also be used to give a stay-at-home parent either occasional or regular time off from the intensive work of child rearing. Parents who are in school also often need to use child care. But the most frequent reason child care is needed is the increased employment of mothers in both married-couple and single-parent households.

Despite the importance of good-quality care for young children, child care that provides a high-quality developmental environment is of little use to parents if they cannot afford it, if the hours do not correspond to their working day, if it is not convenient to either home or workplace, or if it is not reliable. The inability to find child care that meets these criteria and is of sufficient quality can seriously affect parents' peace of mind and, consequently, their performance on the job or their ability to go to work at all. When families can successfully meet their child care needs, both business and society benefit through a more productive work force today and a better prepared one tomorrow. **Child care should be designed to meet the work-related needs of parents as well as the developmental and educational needs of children.**

For many parents, the choice between employment and staying home to care for their children is difficult. Such a decision entails a careful balancing of the benefits and costs of employment, both of which can be considerable. For many mothers, the potential benefits of working are substantial. Many single parents, especially mothers who do not receive child support, earn the only income the family receives.

Although the monetary rewards of maternal employment are not as great for married-couple families as for single mothers, moving from one to two incomes per family was the principal reason that family incomes (adjusted for family type and inflation) rose at all during the 1970s and 1980s, when earnings on average were stagnant.[4] Research has shown that two-earner families have a higher rate of saving[5] and homeownership than single-earner families with equivalent incomes.[6] Other advantages of dual incomes include greater economic stability and a buffer against hardships such as unemployment, illness, death, or divorce.[7] Employment may also bring fringe benefits such as pensions and health insurance, as well as psychological and professional rewards that go beyond monetary compensation.

The decision to work, however, entails the weighing of these benefits against substantial employment-related expenses. After food, housing, and taxes, child care represents the largest single expense for working parents at all income levels,[8] although additional costs accrue in such items as transportation and clothing. But even with these higher work-related expenses, on average the income advantage of dual-earner over single-earner families is still considerable, particularly for low-income families.[9] In this context, however, it is ironic that many families attempting to move off the welfare rolls into self-sufficiency often find working to be too costly. For example, by engaging in paid work, parents who formerly received assistance under Aid to Families with Dependent Children (AFDC) face losing substantial health, child care, and other social service benefits; thus, the cost of working increases in real terms.[10]

Not all costs of working are economic, however; some are psychic. Parents who work often worry that they are not spending enough time with their children[11] or that their child care arrangements are of inferior quality, unreliable, or otherwise not in their children's best interests. These concerns necessitate a major trade-off for many parents who must decide whether the net financial benefits of working are sufficient to justify placing their children in out-of-home care.

STRENGTHENING OUR SOCIETY

Policies that help children develop and parents work may produce additional benefits that accrue to society at large. A more productive work force can mean not only higher wages and business earnings but also a more competitive national economy. Reducing welfare dependency would be a major social achievement. Supporting the institution of the American family and rebuilding some of the "social capital" lost within some families are worthy objectives that can help strengthen the very fabric of society.

Making the Work Force More Productive. Business's interest in improving child care has grown along with its concern for the quality of its current and future work force. Business is facing long-term changes in its pool of labor and shortages in many skill areas. Overall, the work force is becoming older, more ethnically and racially diverse, and more female. Women currently account for 45 percent of the labor force, up dramatically from just under 30 percent in 1950. By the year 2000, women are expected to make up 47 percent of all workers, and the Bureau of Labor Statistics (BLS) expects the labor participation rate of women to exceed 81 percent. Between 1988 and 2000, the BLS projects that women will account for 62 percent of the net growth in the work force.[12] The majority of the women currently in the work force are in their childbearing years, and most will have children during their careers.[13]

Increasingly, business must go beyond traditional employment practices to reach out effectively to a more diverse labor pool. Those companies that have taken steps to address the child care needs of their work force report that they have improved their ability to attract and retain high-quality personnel, thereby enhancing their current work force and their competitiveness. Many businesses also find that helping parents meet their child care needs can potentially reduce absenteeism and employee turnover.[14] The 1990 *National Child Care Survey* (NCCS) found that 15 percent of the mothers in its sample who worked outside the home reported losing some time from work (including arriving late, leaving early, or having to take a full day off) during the previous month because of a failure in their regular child care arrangement.[15] Studies have found that employee turnover produces disruption and inefficiency in the work environment and that the cost of replacing employees is high. For example, Merck & Co., Inc., found that it costs about 1.5 times annual salary to replace a manager and about 75 percent of salary to replace a clerical or technical employee. It also found that it may take considerable time to fill a vacant position and an average of 12.5 months for a new employee to become adjusted to the job.[16]

Many parents, who otherwise would be preoccupied with family problems, can be more effective on the job if they have access to good care for their children. Many companies find that child care and other programs which help employees more effectively balance work and family responsibilities help to raise morale throughout the company, even among employees who do not have children.[17]

Numerous corporations now have considerable experience in creating a variety of options to help parents obtain good-quality care for their children. This experience provides an important base of knowledge for both the private and the public sectors in developing a more coherent approach to child care policy (see Chapter 5).

Reducing Dependency. In addition to providing assistance to parents who are currently working, policy makers have recognized that child care can help reduce welfare dependency by making it increasingly possible for parents to enter or stay in the paid labor force. The Family Support Act (FSA) of 1988 set in motion radical changes in welfare policy by requiring a substantial number of AFDC recipients to either work or go to school in order to continue receiving benefits. In passing this act, Congress recognized that although families should be self-supporting, most welfare recipients who are parents of young children will not be able to work, participate in training, or continue their education unless they are able to find affordable child care.

Building Social Capital. Until fairly recently, five or six was considered the age at which children were mature enough for formal schooling. It was assumed that younger children would receive the necessary nurturing in social and language skills from an intact, multigenerational family in which at least one parent, almost always the mother, stayed at home. Few American families fit this description today.

These profound societal shifts have resulted in a reduction of what University of Chicago sociologist James Coleman calls the "social capital" available to children.[18] He defines "social capital" as "the strength of social relations that make available to the person the resources of others." Like human capital and financial capital, social capital is important for children's educational achievement. Social capital plays a critical role in children's learning, particularly in communicating values and standards of behavior and by providing children with adult attention and involvement, both in the family and in the community. Families have always relied on assistance from relatives, friends, and neighbors; but with the increased labor force participation of women and greater population mobility, these traditional sources of family support are in shorter supply today. For example, data from the NCCS show that between 1965 and 1990, there was a sharp drop in care provided by relatives from 33 to 19 percent. At the same time, care

by unrelated adults increased from 37 to 51 percent, and the use of center-based care grew dramatically from 6 percent to 28 percent.[19]

Increases in dysfunctional families, chaotic communities, single-parent families, and families in which both parents work have reduced the connections among families, communities, schools, and children, limiting the amount of social capital children can draw upon and, in combination with a number of other factors, contributing to a decline in educational achievement overall.[20]

A good-quality child care setting can bolster the social capital of families by providing a stable environment for children that addresses their developmental and educational needs and makes parents feel more secure about the care their children are receiving. Furthermore, child care often links families to other beneficial services from which they might otherwise have been isolated. Society as a whole benefits when its youngest children have the proper health care, early education, and nurturing that will better prepare them for later learning and for life.

Supporting Families. Ensuring the readiness of young children for school and for life requires a full-fledged partnership among families, the community, private-sector institutions (including business and foundations), and the government. Although our American traditions celebrate the power of the individual, we believe that it is the family that provides the foundations upon which our communities are built. Today, those foundations are shaky.

Families of all types need greater societal support to raise their children in today's more complex world. But rather than seeking ways to strengthen all families, many of our public policies have been built on a "deficit model" which insists that families first be in trouble before they can receive help.[21] Too strong an adherence to this approach may undermine the very families we need to strengthen. Families of all types need a variety of community-based supports to enable them to do their primary job of raising their children.

Not all families will need the same level of support. Many families do have access to good support networks among their relatives, friends, and neighbors. But others, such as those headed by young parents, the poor, and many single parents, may need greater access to support services that help improve their parenting skills and attain or maintain a greater degree of self-sufficiency. All families, even the strongest, may at times confront special situations and could benefit from greater access to a variety of family support programs that both provide direct services and help connect families to other community-based resources. Unfortunately, most programs and resources for assisting families are generally fragmented and uncoordinated and are often inflexible. Many families under stress have a hard time locating and gaining access to the social and health services they need. **To improve this situation, we call for more effective integration of social and health services at the community level to provide families with easier access to the services they may need.**

THE CURRENT CHILD CARE SITUATION

WHAT MODERN FAMILIES LOOK LIKE

For most of this century, the typical family was thought to be one in which the mother stayed at home to care for the children while the father worked outside the home. Now, this is hardly the case. In just the fifteen years between 1976 and 1991, the percentage of married couples with children under six in which the father worked and the mother was a homemaker dropped from 55 percent to 34 percent. As a percentage of all families with children under six, such "traditional" families are now just 27 percent, down from 47 percent in 1976.[22]

In the past few decades, dramatic demographic and societal changes have combined to make the traditional model for children's early care less and less common:

- Between 1960 and 1989, the percentage of married women in the labor force with children under the age of six jumped from 18.6 to 58.4 percent.[23]

- In 1992, 52 percent of mothers with children younger than one year old were in the labor force.[24]

- Only 71 percent of children now live in a home headed by a married couple. In 61 percent of married-couple families with children under the age of thirteen, both parents work.[25]

- In 1990, one out of every five children lived in a single-parent family. One of every ten children lived in a household headed by someone other than their own parent, most often a grandmother.[26]

- Women are the head of household in 96 percent of single-parent families. Half of the children in single-mother families are poor, as are almost a quarter in single-father families, even though nearly 70 percent of children in single-parent families have a working parent.[27]

- Although divorce is still responsible for a majority of single-parent homes, more and more children are being born out of wedlock. More than one-quarter of all births in 1990 were to nonmarried mothers, compared with only 4 percent in 1950.[28]

- Seventy percent of children in poverty have parents who work for either all or part of their income. Over 2 million of these children (40 percent) have parents who work and do not receive any public assistance. Surprisingly, fewer than one-third have families whose only source of reported income is public assistance.[29]

These trends mean that a higher percentage of all parents are in the work force than ever before and must depend on some form of child care for their youngest children. A three-year-old in full-time child care may be spending half of his or her waking hours in the care of adults other than his or her parents.

School-age children also need special care arrangements to accommodate the hours beyond the school day, in both the morning and the afternoon, that correspond to their parents' workday.

SHARING RESPONSIBILITY FOR YOUNG CHILDREN

In the United States, we have long maintained that the cost of elementary and secondary education should be assumed by the entire community, through all taxpayers, not just parents. This view is based on the conviction that education is an investment which produces a literate and skilled population, bringing substantial returns to the entire nation, not just the children who are educated and their families. Although the individuals and their families certainly benefit by the greater lifetime earnings that higher levels of education usually confer, society also benefits when its education system produces citizens capable of exercising their civic duties, participating productively in the economy, and fulfilling their adult responsibilities.

There is a great deal more public ambivalence over the issue of responsibility for the care and education of young children before they enter public school. We believe that parents rightfully have the primary responsibility for meeting the developmental and educational needs of children from birth to school age. Unfortunately, not all parents have either the skills or the resources to provide adequate nurturing. And many parents who must work or complete their education feel that they do not have enough time with their children.

A DIVERSE SYSTEM TO MEET DIVERSE NEEDS

Child care in America is best characterized by its diversity. Children are being cared for in a wide variety of settings:

- In their own homes by parents, other relatives, or paid help.
- In the homes of relatives or neighbors.
- In small family child care homes in which a neighborhood woman may care for up to 6 children.
- In child care centers that may be small, with several dozen children, or may enroll in excess of 100. Child care centers may be nonprofit or profit-making and may be independent, part of a chain or network, affiliated with a public school system or religious institution, or maintained by a business for the benefit of its employees.

We believe that the diversity of our society and the differing needs of children and parents argue against a uniform system of care. Families from different ethnic, racial, and religious backgrounds may have special preferences for their children's care and early education. Children have special needs as well. Poor children or those otherwise at risk educationally may need programs that combine comprehensive health and educational services, whereas most nonpoor children from intact two-parent families and many single-parent families may not need more from child care than a nurturing and educational environment.

Although we believe that the needs of children from low-income families and those who have other disadvantages should be targeted first by federal policy, in many communities this has led to a highly stratified care system that reduces rather than enhances diversity. Policies should try to avoid exacerbating existing racial, cultural, and income segregation of children. We believe that such segregation teaches the wrong lessons about separation to children at a very young and vulnerable age and that it is good for children to be exposed to others from a wide spectrum of cultures and family backgrounds. Nevertheless, we recognize that there are many practical considerations, such as the neighborhood-based nature of most child care centers and family child care homes, that make it difficult to substantially integrate many child care facilities. A system that is responsive to community and family needs should try to encourage diversity within programs. Nevertheless, building such a system inevitably will entail trade-offs among needs, benefits, and costs of different care arrangements and how these costs should be shared among key constituencies.

Some good models for more effective delivery of child care services already exist (several are described in detail in Chapter 5). However, because the needs, resources, and character of different communities may vary substantially, we believe that more experimentation will be necessary to find alternative models that work best in particular localities. **We believe that the most workable delivery systems should be adapted to local needs through substantive public-private partnerships that include resources from those who have a stake in improved child care: government, employers, parents, educators, and members of the community.** In many communities, business, which has gained experience in addressing the child care needs of employees and others in the community, can take an important leadership role in developing and sustaining these partnerships.

DIFFICULT CHOICES AHEAD: HOW MUCH? FOR WHOM? WHO PAYS?

The preceding discussion identifies an impressive list of gains that might be achieved by a well-functioning child care system. We would like child care to enhance the well-being of children and working parents, raise the productivity of the work force, and promote social objectives such as building social capital and reducing welfare dependency. Yet, high-quality child care is expensive, and the scarce resources it requires must be taken largely from other private or public uses. As always in the real world, trade-offs between objectives become necessary, and achieving objectives in the most efficient manner is essential.

Our society has always depended on families to put large resources into the care and education of children, but these child-raising activities of the traditional stay-at-home parent or indeed of employed parents, like other household production, are not included in the official GDP statistics. However, the value of this economic activity is extremely large. The total value of all unpaid household work is approximately one-third of conventionally measured GDP; that devoted specifically to the care and education of children might be put at roughly 2 to 4 percent of GDP, on the order of $120 to $240 billion annually.[30] Furthermore, the value of this economic activity may be highest in its least tangible product: the social capital required for society to function peaceably and productively. But in our new "nontraditional" world of changing preferences and more equality and employment opportunities for women, how should the care and raising of children best be accomplished?

The central element of the problem is defined by the observation that "a major impediment to increasing the supply of quality child care is the real cost of providing such care. Child-care fees that seem high to the parents who purchase care are very low from the perspective of child-care providers. More importantly, they are substantially below the full cost of providing high-quality care."[31]

In a pure market system, when a service costs more than consumers are willing or able to pay, it is not produced. By this analysis, if child care costs more than a woman's net earnings and other rewards from employment, the woman's economic value is greatest in the home. This pure market analysis, however, ignores two major factors.

First, it ignores imperfections in the child care market itself that distort market effects, such as poor information and the high transaction costs for families reflected in the difficulty many have in changing providers. An important example is the failure of the private market to finance investments in child care and the associated employment, education, and training that provide long-term economic benefits to children and their mothers. An investment in skills for a relatively unskilled mother may enable her to earn future income that will more than cover the immediate costs of child care, both to her and to society. Similarly, continuity of employment, which child care makes possible, raises the lifetime earnings of women by aiding their career advancement. And for children from low-income families, having a mother in the work force may actually have a positive impact on later educational performance. A recent study by researchers at the University of Wisconsin, Madison, and the University of Texas found that for children from low-income, single-mother families, maternal employment during infancy and the toddler years actually enhances intellectual development in elementary school by providing a more stimulating developmental environment.[32]

Second, the pure market analysis ignores the possibility of significant "external benefits" from child care — benefits that accrue to society at large rather than to consumers and providers. This raises important questions. Does the market, which largely represents the direct interests of child care consumers and providers, therefore produce too little child care? Is there a strong public interest in child care, providing the rationale for public intervention through tax, spending, or regulatory policies? And, in particular, is there a public interest in providing subsidies in some cases to bring affordability into line with costs?

We believe there clearly is such a public interest for many of the reasons discussed earlier in this chapter. First, while most parents undoubtedly want to "do the best for their children," there are additional economic and social benefits to the nation from developing its children into productive workers and citizens, especially when the alternatives involve the costs of social disintegration and crime, physical decay, and heavier tax burdens for social services.

Second, these elements of public interest have additional force in the case of poor children, both because the costs to society of neglecting their development are likely to be higher than for middle-class children and because the American commitment to equal opportunity implies some societal obligation to children whose families cannot or do not provide opportunities for them.

Third, in the Family Support Act of 1988, our society has strongly affirmed the social value of work, apart from its economic value, as a means of reducing welfare dependency. This political decision entails a social and financial commitment to child care that can make such work possible.

The growth of federal and state child care programs and tax relief policies demonstrates that to a certain extent policy makers already recognize society's interest. At the same time, a continuing ambivalence about child care is reflected in the fragmented and uncoordinated way that policy is developed and programs are funded, governed, and regulated. Our public policies have tended to emphasize child care as an individual consumer good and to neglect its function as a public investment that benefits society at large. **We believe that society has a strong interest in helping families to ensure that the care their children receive before they enter school enhances their intellectual, physical, social, and emotional development, whether this is care at home or in a child care setting.**

Unfortunately, listing the benefits of child care and establishing a public interest in them do not answer the hard questions. Even if more scarce resources should be allocated to child care, how many more? How can they be most effectively employed? And, always most difficult, to whom should they go, and who will pay?

Although we have not always been able to provide specific answers to these questions in the analysis and recommendations that follow, we have tried to remain mindful of the difficult choices our recommendations entail. We recognize, for example, that the "correct" outcomes for different families will depend very much on their own preferences, abilities, and circumstances. We note that sometimes public policy should encourage alternatives to child care. For some families, depending on parental preferences and earning capacity, maternal care may be more appropriate than employment supported by heavily subsidized child care, although we must keep in mind the possible long-term benefits of employment and the costs of welfare dependency. And we stress that subsidies for child care should be carefully directed at the critical public interests noted above. There is little to be gained by taxing a middle-class family to subsidize its own child care, and there are certainly limits to the willingness of middle-class families without young children to pay taxes to subsidize the child care of their neighbors.

SUMMARY OF RECOMMENDATIONS

This policy statement addresses a broad set of issues that must inform both public and private decisions on child care. Specifically, it examines the respective roles and responsibilities of business, government, communities, and parents in developing a true public-private partnership to meet the nation's growing child care needs. The statement looks at three critical and interrelated issues:

- The quality of care that is sufficient to address the developmental needs of children
- The availability of decent-quality care
- The affordability of such care for parents and society

Chapter 1 examines the connection between child care and education and how child care affects different sectors in society, and it provides a summary of the statement's key recommendations. Chapter 2 looks at the quality of child care: how it is defined, how it affects development, and its availability. Chapter 3 examines the economics of child care: how much it costs, how much parents pay, and the various government subsidies that help to make it more affordable for parents. Chapter 4 looks at strategies for improving the quality of care available to children and families. Chapter 5 explores the variety of approaches being used by business to address the child care needs of employees as well as several alternative approaches to delivering child care more effectively at the community level.

SETTING PRIORITIES FOR THE CHILD CARE SYSTEM

Any effort to improve the overall quality of the child care system will have to confront the reality that delivering higher-quality care to more children inevitably means higher costs. Unfortunately, it is difficult to determine with certainty how much it might cost to carry out much of the broad agenda we outline in this policy statement and what the specific outcomes will be for the healthier development of children. There are substantial disagreements over the potential trade-offs between costs and benefits in various areas. For example, a number of studies indicate that a comprehensive and sustained approach to early childhood care and education has substantial benefits for the long-term educational success of disadvantaged children.[33] The data on the long-term benefits of high-quality child care for non-disadvantaged children are considerably less conclusive. Numerous studies on child care quality indicate that group size, staff-to-child ratio, and caregiver training and compensation have an impact on children in center-based care, but there is little certainty about the precise levels of program resources needed to assure children's proper development.

The lack of hard data on what constitutes sufficient care quality for most children complicates efforts to estimate what good care should cost. Current estimates for good-quality center-based care for three- to five-year-olds vary widely, ranging from $4,900 per year to $8,300, depending on the level of staff compensation, which is one of the key parameters for improving quality. Other factors that complicate efforts to accurately assess costs are the considerably higher cost of infant and toddler care and substantial regional cost variations. It is therefore difficult to know with any certainty how much it would cost to provide higher-quality care to all children currently in child care centers, much less to the additional children whose mothers might enter the work force if affordable quality care were more available.

A number of recent national studies underscore the problems of the child care system. Nevertheless, a major barrier to developing practical solutions is the lack of hard data on such critical issues as how many children are now receiving inadequate services, how many more children may need to be served in the future, the extent to which stronger regulations may affect the supply and cost of care, how much providing additional quality would cost, and which trade-offs are most acceptable among the program characteristics that affect quality. **We recommend that the federal government, foundations, universities, and research institutions give data collection and cost-benefit analysis of child care a very high priority.**

Despite the obvious lack of sufficient data, improving child care and early childhood education will clearly continue to be a critical issue. We believe there are key problem areas within child care that deserve attention from policy makers in the near term. CED recognizes that the nation and its communities currently lack the resources — either financial or human — to tackle all these problems simultaneously or, indeed, quickly. Some of the quality improvements we recommend would require greater funding, but others require almost no additional outlays. The key question is whether higher costs in some areas will be justified by the benefits that higher-quality care will bring to the development and education of children, to their parents, and ultimately, to the education system, to business, and to society. **We believe that in the long term, a greater investment in improved education and care of young children will be justified but that the reality of limited resources in the near future demands that we carefully establish priorities based on the projected benefits and costs of different child care policies.**

Building a child care system that does a better job of serving both the short-term and the long-term interests of children, parents, business, education, and society will require more coherent and comprehensive programs and policies. We believe that the recommendations discussed in the sections that follow should receive the highest priority and be addressed as soon as feasible.

HELPING LOW-INCOME FAMILIES

We urge the federal government to give its highest priority to meeting the child care needs of low-income children and families. Low-income disadvantaged children are the most in need of care that meets their developmental and educational needs but are the least likely to get it. At the same time, society has an enormous stake in helping low-income parents enter and remain in the work force so that their families can become self-sufficient. A combination of strategies will be necessary to better meet the child care needs of low-income children and their families.

- **Federal child care subsidies should be distributed more equitably to provide a greater proportion of financial assistance to lower-income, rather than higher-income, families.*** This means making the dependent care tax credit (DCTC) refundable so that low-income families are eligible for the maximum benefit even if they do not have a tax liability.

- **Federal child care subsidies should be adjusted to provide proportionately more funds directly to programs.** Such supply-side subsidies have been shown to have a greater impact on improving child care quality in centers that serve low-income children than consumer subsidies such as the DCTC. We also encourage the use of a blended strategy of direct provider subsidies and vouchers to parents to help encourage both improved child care quality and greater choice in selecting a program for their child.

- **The access of low-income working parents to full-day high-quality child care should be improved by expanding Head Start to include more full-day programs and by coordinating Head Start with the**

---

*See memorandum by OWEN B. BUTLER (page 68).

Family Support Act child care programs. Restructuring is needed at the federal and state levels to coordinate the various programs created to provide care and education for low-income children (such as Head Start, FSA-approved child care, and other community-based child care services). This will allow families to gain greater access to the comprehensive, full-day care their children need. In particular, it should be possible for these programs to combine federal and state funding sources more easily so that more Head Start and other preschool programs would be able to provide full-day care at a single site.

- **More attention should be paid to the quality of Head Start programs to ensure that children receive the developmental benefits the program was designed to deliver.** We support continued progress toward the full-funding targets established by Congress when Head Start was reauthorized in 1990, but we believe that expanding enrollment should not be accomplished at the expense of program quality. We urge that a portion of any new Head Start funds should be earmarked to improve quality and salaries and provide more full-day services.

- **Disadvantaged preschoolers should have access to sustained intervention efforts through more follow-through programs in elementary schools.** The new Head Start Transition Project, which is the first follow-up program to provide the full range of Head Start services through the third grade, is a good beginning.

IMPROVING STAFF COMPENSATION AND TRAINING

We urge upgrading the compensation and training of child care staff in order to improve the general quality of care. The quality of the relationship between the child and the caregiver is the most important determinant of how well a child thrives in child care. Appropriate training of caregivers has a positive effect on that relationship. The very low level of child care wages (an average of $11,500 for preschool teachers in child care centers[34]), on the other hand, results in high turnover, compromising the child-caregiver relationship and reducing the reliability of services for parents.

IMPROVING FAMILY CHILD CARE HOMES

Improving the quality of family child care homes should have a high priority. We recommend the use of a variety of community-based strategies for upgrading this important form of child care, including the expansion and improvement of resource and referral agencies and the development of networks of family care homes, which can offer providers greater access to a variety of educational resources, training opportunities, and professional interaction. About 4 million children, or half of all children in out-of-home care, are in family child care homes. This is where infants and toddlers are more likely to be. Family care is generally more affordable than center-based care. However, more than three-quarters of family child care homes are unlicensed and unregulated. As a result, little is known about their quality. There are a number of low-cost ways to upgrade family child care homes, including establishing community-based networks that enable family care providers to have professional contact with others in their field, provide access to a variety of educational resources, and provide information on available financial assistance. Mobile resource services can bring training and educational resources directly to participating family providers, and additional training opportunities can be offered at local colleges or other community-based institutions.

IMPROVING CARE FOR INFANTS AND TODDLERS

We recommend placing a high priority on developing more effective strategies for addressing the special child care needs of infants and toddlers. Infant and toddler care, particularly for children under the age of one, is the area of fastest demand growth. It is also the most expensive, often costing one-third more than child care for older preschoolers. Therefore, much of the need is going unmet, and much of the quality of existing infant care is less than adequate. Unfortunately, the high cost of good-quality infant care means that there are no easy solutions for closing the gap.

Among other provisions, the 1993 Family and Medical Leave Act recently passed into law mandates that companies with more than fifty employees provide twelve weeks of unpaid parental leave for the birth or adoption of a child. Although we support the principle of parental leave, we do not believe that these mandates should be extended to smaller businesses. We believe that smaller businesses need flexibility in addressing personnel issues if they are to be competitive and that the costs of rigid leave policies to small businesses are not adequately understood. In lieu of extending mandates, we would favor tax-based incentives to companies to encourage them to provide leave to parents following the birth or adoption of an infant. A combination of more widespread availability of parental leave policies and greater flexibility in job scheduling for new parents would help to alleviate some of the need for out-of-home infant care. Unfortunately, many parents cannot afford to take an unpaid leave even if that option were more available. Given the growing demand for quality infant care services and the high cost of those services, a concerted effort is needed by government, business, and community leaders to identify strategies for expanding the supply of affordable, qualified providers.

IMPROVING INFORMATION FOR FAMILIES

We strongly recommend improving the access of all parents to better information and assistance in finding quality child care. Parents need better information on which to base their child care choices, help in locating good-quality programs in their community, and help in gaining access to available financial assistance. These goals can be accom-plished through public education programs and improved community-based resource and referral agencies.

IMPROVING CHILD CARE STANDARDS

We urge states and localities to develop standards for child care that promote the health and safety of children and support improved child care quality but that are not intrusive and do not place an unreasonable burden of compliance on child care providers. Because children cannot protect themselves and parents cannot always monitor what is happening to their children when they are away from home, we believe there is an overriding public stake in protecting the health and safety of young children in out-of-home care. However, we believe the states and localities are in the best position to adopt reasonable health, safety, and quality standards that do not place an undue burden on providers at the local level. We encourage states to develop performance standards that reflect current professional knowledge of the characteristics that promote positive outcomes for young children in out-of-home care but that allow providers flexibility in meeting the standards. We also believe federal funding for programs for low-income children should be contingent on compliance with state standards.

*   *   *

Building a coherent system of child care will require a sustained partnership among all those who stand to benefit: parents, educators, employers, and the larger community. Federal and state policy makers need to take the lead in addressing the issue of affordability for low- and moderate-income parents and in helping to create an infrastructure for child care services on which communities can build. At the same time, business has an overriding interest in this issue, and it should continue to provide leadership both locally and nationally by forging partnerships and helping to develop workable strategies for meeting the early care and education needs of children and families.

Chapter 2

IDENTIFYING QUALITY CHILD CARE

By focusing the first of the nation's six education goals on school readiness, the President and the nation's governors acknowledged that far too many children reach school age without the skills to succeed in formal education. But ensuring a child's readiness for school is no simple task. The report of the National Task Force on School Readiness notes that readiness involves a complex set of factors that include far more than academic knowledge and skills; more important are children's physical health, self-confidence, and social competence.[1]

Although it may be difficult to quantify exactly what determines a child's readiness for school, one thing can be said with certainty: Children do not wait until formal schooling to begin to learn. Learning is a lifelong process that starts at birth, and many of the preconditions for brain development and physical health are set before birth.

In the first few years of life, children are learning about themselves and the world around them through their interactions with the environment and the adults and other children in their lives. What children learn and how well they learn it depend on the ability of parents and other caregivers to provide the nurturing, emotional stability, and intellectual stimulation children need to continue on a healthy course of development.

With so many more children now in full-day nonparental care, a growing proportion of early childhood education is taking place in a variety of settings, not just in traditional part-day nursery schools and preschools or at home. Therefore, it is essential to focus on the quality of the child care programs in which children are spending so much of their time. This is particularly important for the 25 to 40 percent of young children who enter school educationally disadvantaged by poverty, family problems, abuse, neglect, race, or limited proficiency in English.[2]

In their first five years, all children need the kind of care that helps them develop effective language and other intellectual skills, social skills, and the ability to continue to learn. These are the factors that will put them on the road to success in school and in later life. This is true whether children are being cared for by their parents, by other relatives, or in other formal or informal arrangements.

DEFINING CHILD CARE QUALITY

Quality in child care is determined by the set of interdependent characteristics that will produce the positive outcomes for young children that will make them successful in school and later life. We define "quality" child care as that which provides a nurturing, safe, and stimulating environment for children — care that promotes the positive development of both their minds and their bodies. Although such care can take place in any setting, including a child's own home, in this policy statement we are primarily concerned with the quality of out-of-home settings, particularly child care centers and family child care homes.

The most important aspect of quality is the relationship between the child and the care provider. Ideally, this should be a caring, safe, and stable relationship in which the child learns

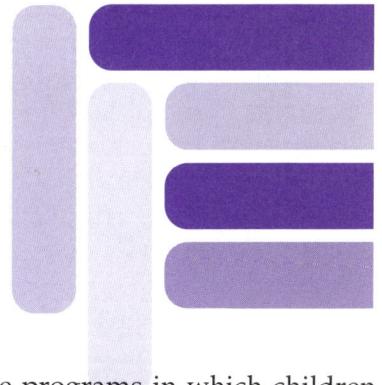

13

about himself or herself and how to get along well with others. Research on the quality of child care has tried to identify a set of characteristics that promote a better adult-child relationship and, as a consequence, more positive outcomes for children.[3]

However, because of the limitations of the research on quality, much of which has been conducted on nonrepresentative samples of children in the context of very high-quality programs, there is no definitive agreement on the levels of these characteristics that are required to promote optimal child development.[4] A number of these studies, which are often cited for demonstrating the long-term benefits of early childhood intervention, such as the Perry Preschool Project, have focused on highly disadvantaged children. This limits their applicability to child care programs for middle-class children.

However, a newer wave of research has been examining child care quality and how it affects more representative groups of children over time in actual community-based programs. Overall, this research is finding that differences in quality as measured by both the interactions of children with caregivers and the structural characteristics of programs have a measurable impact on the development of young children.[5] Nevertheless, the National Research Council (NRC) report on child care cautions that this research has yet to yield definitive answers to the question of which variations in program characteristics produce the desired developmental outcomes.[6]

Despite the limitations of existing research, there is a consensus among both academic researchers and professional practitioners on six criteria that promote better outcomes for children in center-based care.[7]

- **Staff-child ratio:** Staff-child ratios that vary by age of the children and range from no more than 1:4 for infants, 1:3 to 1:6 for toddlers, and 1:7 to 1:10 for preschoolers
- **Group size:** Maximum group sizes in centers that range from 6 to 8 for infants, 6 to 12 for toddlers, and 16 to 20 for preschoolers

- **Caregiver qualifications:** Caregiver education that includes training in child development
- **Caregiver stability and continuity:** Stability and continuity in the relationship between caregiver and child, particularly in a setting where there are multiple caregivers
- **Structure and content of daily activities:** Activities that are structured but allow flexibility so that children can make choices
- **Space and facilities:** Organized and orderly space, with well-differentiated areas for different activities and age groups of children; in family child care, space that is child-oriented

The professional standards developed by the National Association for the Education of Young Children (NAEYC) to accredit child care programs include these structural features but go beyond them to focus on the quality of both the verbal and the nonverbal interactions between caregiver and child, which are strongly associated with children's language and cognitive development.[8] This accreditation program includes a number of criteria to guide the relationships between staff and children and staff and parents: the requirements that staff members interact frequently with children; express respect for and affection toward children; be available and responsive to children; encourage children to share experiences, ideas, and feelings; and listen to them with attention and respect. In addition, NAEYC accreditation requires child care centers to welcome parents to observe the program, discuss policy, make suggestions, and participate in the program.[9]

IMPACT OF CHILD CARE QUALITY ON CHILD DEVELOPMENT

The quality of the interactions between caregiver and child is the strongest predictor of children's language and later intellectual development. The quality and nature of caregivers' speech are particularly important for language development, and research shows that children clearly profit from a verbally stimulating environment in which adults talk frequently with them.[10] Children also gain in cognitive development when caregivers provide more individualized attention, manage activities in a structured way, and engage in more social interaction with the children.[11]

The characteristics of child care settings with which research has most closely associated these outcomes are group size, staff-to-child ratio, caregiver training, and stability of the caregiver-child relationship. Beyond the characteristics of child care programs themselves, however, it is also worth considering how the interaction between family and child care may affect how well children develop.

Group Size. Research on group size indicates that it has a significant effect on children's intellectual development. In one study, children in smaller groups made greater gains on the Preschool Inventory (PSI), an index of school readiness.[12] Numerous studies have found that larger group sizes, in both child care centers and family child care homes, produce fewer positive interactions between caregivers and children.[13]

Staff-to-Child Ratio. Although the evidence on the importance of the staff-to-child ratio for the development of preschoolers is mixed, this characteristic appears to be very important for the development of infants and toddlers.[14] An individual adult is capable of interacting in a sensitive and stimulating way with only a limited number of children at one time. The majority of studies on staff ratios indicate that when adults have fewer children to care for, children's verbal performance improves.[15]

Caregiver Training. Training in child development was associated in both the *National Day Care Study* (NDCS, 1979) and the *National Day Care Home Study* (NDCHS, 1981) with better interactions between caregivers and children, particularly for preschoolers. Other studies point to the importance of a higher level of general education, rather than specific training in child development, for yielding more positive caregiver interactions, particularly with infants.[16]

Caregiver Stability. Multiple changes in child care arrangements have been found to have negative effects on children, including creating less secure attachment to the mother and lower levels of complexity in play. Stable care has been associated with positive longer-term development and better school adjustment in the first grade.[17] Closely connected to the stability of care and the rate of staff turnover is the low level of wages prevalent in the child care industry. The 1990 *National Child Care Staffing Study* (NCCSS) found that staff wages were the most important predictor of both overall child care quality and rate of caregiver turnover.[18]

Role of Parents. Parental involvement may be another important factor for the success of children in child care. We know from research on learning that parents who have more education tend to have children who do better educationally and that parents who read to their young children and who encourage their children to read tend to have children with higher literacy skills. A number of successful early childhood family literacy programs, including Parents as Teachers, the Kenan Trust Family Literacy Project, and the Home Instruction Program for Preschool Youngsters (HIPPY), are based on this premise. However, the NRC notes that although parental involvement may be an important variable in care quality, its implications have not been adequately studied.[19]

BENEFITS OF EARLY CHILDHOOD INTERVENTION FOR DISADVANTAGED CHILDREN

Much of the debate on school readiness has centered on the benefits of redressing the educational and social deficits of disadvantaged three- and four-year-olds through participation in high-quality preschool. The benefits of long-term intervention for their educational and social success have been shown to be significant for children from low-income and welfare-dependent families. Yet, middle- and upper-income children, whether or not their mothers work outside the home, are much more likely to participate in some form of formal preschool education than poor children are. Fewer than half of the children from families that earn less than $30,000 per year are enrolled in preschool, compared with 75 percent of children from families with incomes over $75,000 (see Figure 1).[20]

Studies of the long-term benefits of Head Start and similar programs have shown that these programs gave an immediate boost to children's intellectual performance but that such gains in IQ and achievement test scores can be transitory, fading out by third grade.[21] However, a recent reevaluation of the effectiveness of Head Start and other preschool intervention experiments contends that IQ is a poor measure of cognitive ability and that flaws in control group assignment and testing procedures are at least partly responsible for the apparent fade-out effect.[22] A number of other studies have shown sustainable advantages from preschool intervention. A Cornell University study of eleven preschool and Head Start programs found that after six to thirteen years, program participants were less likely to repeat a grade or be assigned to special education.

The Perry Preschool Project, the most famous of the intervention experiments, found substantial cognitive, social, and economic benefits for both the individual participants and society.[23] The Perry Preschool researchers estimated that every $1.00 invested in the program returned between $4.75 and $6.00 over the lifetime of the children in terms of lower welfare, criminal justice, and remedial education costs and the higher earnings and taxes paid by project participants.

The Perry Preschool program, however, was highly intensive, and its experimental and control groups were small, involving only 123 participants from 57 families. Each of the children was substantially below average in IQ, and few of the mothers worked. Also, the study was conducted at a time before drug and crime problems in poor neighborhoods had escalated to the level at which they now disrupt the lives of children and families. It is therefore questionable whether the Perry Preschool results can be obtained from less comprehensive programs or from child care for nondisadvantaged children. In spite of these qualifications, however, it is significant that an intensive intervention program such as Perry Preschool can have meaningful effects even if it cannot eliminate all the disadvantages of being born into poverty.[24]

Sustained intervention seems to be the key to lasting results for disadvantaged children. At least two recent studies of Head Start-type preschool programs indicate that such interventions need to be begun at an early age and maintained through at least the early elementary grades for the effects to be sustained.[25] One such study examined the impact of preschool on the school readiness of over 4,500

Figure 1

Preschool Enrollment by Family Income

Family Income	Percent of Three- to Five-Year-Olds in Preschool
$10,000 or Less	42%
$10,001 to $20,000	40%
$20,001 to $30,000	41%
$30,001 to $40,000	48%
$40,001 to $50,000	55%
$50,001 to $75,000	60%
More than $75,000	75%

NOTE: Excludes those enrolled in kindergarten and includes those enrolled in nursery schools, prekindergarten programs, and Head Start; also includes three- to five-year-olds with disabilities.
SOURCE: National Center for Education Statistics, *The National Education Goals Report: Building a Nation of Learners* (Washington, D.C.: National Education Goals Panel, 1992), p. 69.

children who were identified as at risk of failure in first grade. The study found that those children who participated in at least three years of preschool were as prepared for school as a control group of children who were identified as not at risk. At the same time, children judged to be at risk who received only one or two years of preschool still lagged behind in measures of school readiness.[26]

Another recent study, conducted in several Chicago schools by researchers from Loyola University, highlights the fact that elementary school programs are rarely designed to address the comprehensive needs of disadvantaged children or to build on the learning foundations developed by programs such as Head Start. Most preschool intervention programs have little continuity or follow-through once the children enter school. In the Loyola study, the researchers found significant achievement gains in Head Start children who received intensive follow-up in specially designed "Child Parent Centers" during their elementary school years, although there were significant differences in the amount of follow-up required by girls and boys. The study found that to sustain the achievement gains of Head Start, girls need four to six years of intensive extra help following Head Start and that boys, who are much more susceptible to peer pressure, need seven to nine years.[27]

WHAT IS THE QUALITY OF CHILD CARE GENERALLY?

Extensive surveys of quality in center-based child care, including the NDCS, the NCCSS, and *A Profile of Child Care Settings* (PCCS, 1991), have found a mixed picture of quality in center-based care nationally. The NCCSS study found that in the decade following the NDCS, child care centers tended to be larger, received fewer government funds, were more likely to be for-profit operations, and cared for a larger proportion of infants. The NCCSS reported more teachers with some college training but fewer with bachelor's or graduate degrees. It also found that ratios of children to staff have increased but that group sizes have declined. The PCCS, on the other hand, found that both child-to-staff ratios and group sizes had increased. It also found that although the majority of directors of center-based programs reported that their programs met state regulations, their average group sizes and child-staff ratios approached the top of the ranges recommended by early childhood professionals.

The NCCSS found that in the majority of the fifty-seven centers it studied, quality was barely adequate. Overall, the biggest concern was the high turnover rate of the teaching staff, which had risen from 15 percent per year in 1977 to 41 percent in 1988. The NCCSS found that children in centers with lower quality and higher staff turnover were less competent in language and social development. The study also found that the most important predictor of staff turnover was wages, with turnover twice as high among staff earning $4 or less per hour (54 percent) than among those earning more than $6 per hour (27 percent). (The average hourly wage of child care staff was $5.35; when adjusted for inflation, this represents a decrease of more than 20 percent since 1977.) This suggests, the NCCSS researchers note, that "dollars spent on staff wages are dollars well spent on creating stable environments for children." [28]

The NCCSS also looked at the differences in quality indicators between child care centers run under different auspices: nonprofits, church-related nonprofits, and for-profits, both independents and chains. Overall quality tends to be highest among nonprofits and lowest among for-profits, particularly judged by staff turnover, staff education, and level of developmentally appropriate activities. It also found that middle-income children were disproportionately represented in for-profit centers, whereas both higher- and lower-income children were more frequently enrolled in higher-quality nonprofit care.[29]

Most of the studies on quality have focused on center-based care. As many young children, approximately 4 million, are enrolled in family child care homes as in centers. Less is known about the overall quality of family care homes, largely because most are not licensed or regulated in any way, and therefore reliable data are difficult to obtain. However, at least one extensive Canadian study that included family care homes found that quality was much more variable in family care and that this variable quality had a more notice-able effect on children's language development than quality differences in center-based care did.[30]

As we discuss in Chapter 3, the full cost of high-quality child care is high, and attempting to attain the smallest possible group sizes and high staff-child ratios simultaneously with the best possible caregiver qualifications and stability and other indicators of quality may be prohibitively expensive for both parents and

---

MEETING THE NEEDS OF CHILDREN IN FRANCE

The experience of France in developing a national child care system provides an instructive example of how another industrialized nation views the importance of early child-hood development. The French system is based on the belief that every child benefits from working and playing cooperatively with other children under skilled adult supervision. The French point to national census data showing that children of any social class have a better chance of passing first grade — a critical indicator of later school success — if they have attended preschool.

Recognizing that most parents cannot afford the full cost of quality child care, the French government has chosen to subsidize the portion that exceeds parents' means. Nearly 80 percent of the cost of child care is covered by public funds. Free preschools serve nearly 90 percent of all three-, four-, and five-year-olds, and publicly subsidized private schools serve the remainder. The total yearly cost per pupil for preschool is $2,100, which includes basic program costs of teachers' salaries and buildings as well as a "wraparound" program that provides care to children before and after preschool, at lunchtime, and during vacations. Parents pay only $210 to cover the cost of the wraparound; the rest is paid for by public funding.

Several types of infant-toddler care are available, including centers, family child care networks, and independent licensed family child care providers. Teachers and other professional staff are aggressively recruited and receive intensive training. All preschool teachers and directors have training equivalent to a master's degree in early childhood and elementary education. Directors of infant-toddler programs are pediatric nurses who have professional training in public health, child development, and administration. An extensive national system of preventive health care for mothers and their infants has reduced France's infant mortality rate to the world's tenth lowest. (By contrast, the United States ranks twenty-third.) Systematic links between health care services and children's programs help ensure that every child in infant-toddler and preschool care receives regular preventive health care.

In 1988, France spent 56.8 billion francs on child care and development programs for children under the age of six. If this were scaled to the size of the U.S. population, the expenditure would be equivalent to $34.8 billion (in 1988 dollars). In that same year, the United States spent approximately $16.6 billion on such programs, including $9.6 billion for public kindergartens, $1.5 billion for Head Start, and $5.5 billion for other child care-related programs.

SOURCE: Gail Richardson and Elizabeth Marx, *A Welcome for Every Child: How France Achieves Quality in Child Care* (New York: French-American Foundation, 1989), and Barbara R. Bergmann, "Can We Afford to Save Our Children?: Cost and Structure of Government Programs for Children in the U.S. and France" (Working papers, Department of Economics, American University, Washington, D.C., 1992).

society (see Chapter 3, pages 23-24). Trade-offs between different determinants of quality therefore become necessary, and different families, groups, or communities may prefer different solutions.

France provides an interesting example of how another society deals with this problem. The French have decided to trade off larger group size and higher child-staff ratios for a cadre of relatively well-compensated child care teachers with a high level of education and training. In French *écoles maternelles*, there are typically twenty-eight children per class with one teacher per classroom and one aide who is shared by every two classrooms.

WHAT PARENTS LOOK FOR IN CHILD CARE

In surveys, parents invariably indicate that the most important characteristic they want in child care is quality.[31] However, parents tend to use different criteria to judge quality than professionals do.[32] Although both parents and professionals associate quality with the relationship between the child and the care provider, parents of infants and toddlers are less concerned with licensing or the level of training of the caregivers, characteristics that professionals value because research has generally shown them to be correlated with the kind of warm, caring relationships that parents desire.[33] For preschoolers, however, parents usually define quality child care as care that has greater educational content and consider this a top priority.[34]

According to focus groups conducted for Dayton Hudson Corporation, parents do not even feel comfortable discussing child care quality. This project found that parents tend to feel guilty if they must place their child in a setting that is only adequate because they cannot afford what professionals tell them is higher quality.[35] Studies of child care preferences suggest that about two-thirds of parents say they are satisfied with their child care arrangement but that one-third would prefer something else.[36]

Ironically, parents do not necessarily pay more for higher quality. They often pay the same for care of widely differing quality, as measured by staff-child ratios, group size, and caregiver training, despite the fact that quality as measured by these professional criteria is generally highly correlated with actual program costs.[37] This results from several factors. First, the variety of supply- and demand-side subsidies masks the true cost of quality care. Second, program directors are reluctant to raise rates even as costs go up because they fear that parents will not be willing or able to pay more. Third, parents generally have little information on which to base their decisions, and they often choose care based more on price, convenient location, and hours than on professional definitions of quality.[38]

WHO GETS QUALITY CARE?

In the absence of government subsidies to lower-income families, higher-quality child care and higher socioeconomic status would naturally seem to go together. However, given current subsidy arrangements, the NDCS found that centers serving children from low-income, single-parent families that received federal funding provided higher-quality settings in the form of better staff-child ratios.[39] This conclusion is also supported by the NCCSS, which indicated that poor and wealthy children had access to better center-based care than children from moderate-income families did.[40] In contrast, a number of studies indicate that families under greater social and psychological stress or whose lives were more complex (circumstances that included parents who live apart or who work split shifts, weekends, or long hours) tend to use lower-quality center care, whereas families with a nurturing and supportive social network had children in higher-quality settings.[41]

WHAT IS THE AVAILABILITY OF QUALITY CARE?

According to the PCCS, the majority of center-based programs report group sizes and child-staff ratios that meet both state regulations and professional recommendations. The same is true of regulated home-based providers.[42] Nevertheless, meeting state regulations does not guarantee adequate quality. Regulations vary substantially from state to state; and many programs, such as preschools run by religious organizations and family child care homes with fewer than three or four children, are exempted. This leaves open the possibility of large variations in quality among providers both within and among states. There is substantial evidence from the NCCSS and other surveys that although the total number of child care slots has kept up with demand, the quality of the child care available in many areas is uneven. The cost of care that meets professional standards is generally more than most parents feel able or willing to pay (see Chapter 3 for a more detailed discussion of this issue). Here the issue is not so much a shortage of child care in an economic sense as a question of whether parents or society should be willing to pay more because they are currently undervaluing the benefits for children and society of higher-quality and presumably more expensive care; such a situation would be likely to result in the underproduction of quality care.

There seem to be real shortages, however, in specialized care areas, such as infant and toddler care, care for handicapped children, sick-child care, and care during nontraditional hours. These services are necessarily more expensive to provide and are often out of the range of affordability for most parents.[43] Therefore, fewer providers have entered the market, and access to care at any price may be a much more severe problem.

Chapter 3

THE ECONOMICS OF CHILD CARE:
Meeting the Growing Demands
of Families and Society

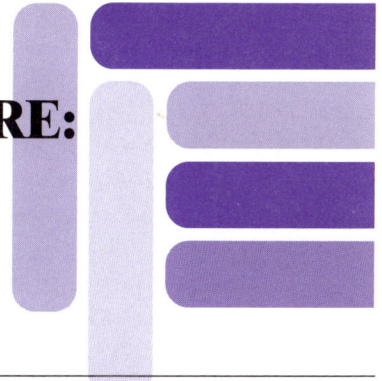

Before policy decisions can be made on what would be appropriate to invest in higher child care quality, it is important to understand how much is currently being spent, what better-quality care would cost, what new resources may be needed to address our priority concerns, and what trade-offs between quality and cost could legitimately be made. The most problematic barrier to raising child care quality is that higher quality generally costs more to deliver.

A wide number of existing federal and state programs are designed to improve the affordability of nonparental care for young children. Some are tax-based, others give direct subsidies to providers, and still others offer vouchers to low-income parents so that they can choose whatever provider they wish. The nation spends approximately $23 billion annually on child care. The federal government provides more than $9 billion of that each year for a variety of programs, and many states provide additional subsidies to low-income parents. In the private sector, a growing number of businesses assist their employees to some degree with the cost of child care to help make it more affordable. Many private and community foundations also contribute to reducing child care costs for parents.

Despite the proliferation of federal and state programs, there are serious questions about whether the financial benefits of various tax-based programs are reaching the families and children who need assistance the most and whether current government policies have a positive impact on the quality of care.

WHAT PARENTS SPEND

What parents spend on child care varies widely, depending on employment status, income, and type of arrangement. Surprisingly, a sizable proportion (44 percent) of mothers who are employed full time or part time pay nothing for child care, relying instead on relatives and spouses. However, 68 percent of mothers who are employed full time do pay for child care.[1]

In 1990, the average fee paid by parents was approximately $3,173 per year for full-time center-based care and $2,565 in a family child care home.[2] However, the average cost obscures the substantial variation in fees and subsidies among child care settings, classes of income, and regions of the country.[3] The national average for what mothers employed full time spend on child care is $68 per week, according to the *National Child Care Survey* (NCCS). For employed parents in the Boston area, however, the average weekly expenditure is $130 per week.[4] It is estimated that parents' fees pay for, on average, about 76 percent of the cost of center-based care.[5]

Low-income families (those earning less than $15,000) are more likely to use relatives or extended community networks for child care, which, on average, keeps their child care expenses lower. However, these lower costs still represent a higher proportion of income.[6] Among low-income parents who pay for child care, the expenditure consumes an average of 22 to 25 percent of family income, an amount equivalent to the average family expenditure on housing. Moderate-income families (those earning between $15,000 and $25,000) spend about 12 to 13 percent of their income on child care. As family income rises, a lower percentage is spent on child care. Families that earn more than $50,000 spend just 6 percent (see Figure 1).[7] The level of resources it takes to pay for child care also varies significantly for single- versus two-parent families. Single mothers spend 21 percent of their income on average, whereas two-parent families spend 9 percent.[8]

Parents often are not aware of exactly how much they are paying for their children's care. When asked to calculate what they spend, parents rarely deduct the amount they receive through federal or state tax subsidies. According to calculations by the Families and Work Institute, families that actually pay for child care in cash spent approximately $13.6 billion on all forms of care in 1990 (see Figure 2). In that same year, the dependent care tax credit (DCTC) returned approximately $4.0 billion to parents. If that is subtracted from the amount parents said they spent, the true parental contribution in cash was closer to $9.6 billion. Other federal subsidies amounted to approximately $5.5 billion (see Figure 4, page 27), bringing the total spent on child care by par-

(see Figure 4, page 27)

Figure 1

Percentage of Family Income Spent on Child Care

Family Income	Percent Spent on Child Care[a]
$14,999 or Less	23%
$15,000 to $24,999	12%
$25,000 to $34,999	8%
$35,000 to $49,999	7%
$50,000 or More	6%

[a] Mean percentage of family income spent on child care by employed mothers, with youngest child under age five, who pay for care.

SOURCE: *National Child Care Survey* (1990).

Figure 2

What Parents Spend in Cash on Different Forms of Care for Children Under Five
(in billions)

Type of Care	Mother Employed	Mother Not Employed	Total
Centers	$5.90	$1.34	$7.24
Family Child Care	3.61	0.66	4.27
Relatives	1.13	[a]	1.13
In-Home Care	0.74	0.21	0.95
Total	$11.38	$2.21	$13.59

[a] Sample size too small to provide accurate amount; does not affect total.

SOURCE: Ellen Galinsky and Dana Friedman, *Education Before School: Investing in Quality Child Care,* A Study Prepared for the Committee for Economic Development (New York: Scholastic Inc., 1993), p. 99.

ents and the federal government to approximately $19.1 billion.

A recent analysis of child care expenditures by William Prosser and Sharon McGroder of the Department of Health and Human Services found a one-third increase in total child care expenditures between 1975 and 1990 as measured in constant 1990 dollars.[9] This analysis puts the total child care market for 1990 at $23 billion. It is likely that this increase represents greater utilization of care in terms of the number of children served and the average number of hours in care, rather than an increase in the cost to parents for the care of an individual child. Prosser and McGroder found that despite the increase in total child care expenditures between 1975 and 1990, the average amount families spent remained nearly constant at approximately $2,550.[10] Other studies confirm this. The NCCS found that after adjusting for inflation, the hourly costs of center-based and family child care remained relatively stable between 1975 and 1990,[11] while *A Profile of Child Care Settings* (PCCS) found a moderate 5 percent increase in the cost of family child care and no increase in center costs.[12]

THE FULL PRODUCTION COST OF QUALITY CARE

Calculating the true cost of quality child care is difficult. The average price parents pay represents only a fraction of child care's full production cost. Numerous subsidies, including financial and in-kind (for example, the common use of churches or community facilities for nonprofit centers), mask true production costs and sometimes contribute to resource inequities among low-, moderate-, and high-income families.

Many factors may affect the cost of care, including location, type of setting, and age of children, with infant and toddler care generally costing more than care for three- and four-year-olds. Many centers subsidize the higher cost of infant care through higher tuition rates for older preschoolers. Although parents' hourly expenditures have remained relatively constant, a number of researchers contend that the actual full production cost of providing care of a *constant quality* has increased but that providers are hesitant to raise fees beyond what they believe parents are willing or able to pay.[13] Since staff salaries and benefits account for an average of 62 percent of the budgets of all programs,[14] providers who seek to keep fees down generally must do so by keeping labor costs low.

Consistent with this view, there is evidence of a substantial decline since the mid-1970s in the real earnings of both family child care providers and teachers in centers.[15] The generally low wages of child care staff contribute to the high turnover rate experienced by most care programs. Since high staff turnover has been associated with poor developmental outcomes for children, the low and declining earnings of caregivers raise a serious issue for child care quality. The PCCS estimated that about 50 percent of programs experience turnover in any one year; of those, the average turnover rate for staff is also 50 percent. Average teacher turnover in all programs is about 25 percent.[16]

There are several reasons why the child care market produces the low caregiver compensation associated with high turnover. On the demand side, there may be a lack of understanding by parents and society of the value for children of caregiver stability and qualifications. With respect to supply, caregivers consider factors other than compensation. In part, the low wages may be explained by the part-time nature of child care employment and other positive features of child care work; some workers may be willing to accept low wages in exchange for the flexibility of a part-time position and the implicit enjoyment of working with young children.[17] Regardless of the reason for low child care salaries, higher compensation of child care staff will be necessary to reduce the high turnover rates in both centers and family care that lower program quality.

What does high-quality child care really cost? In 1990, the General Accounting Office (GAO) estimated the annual cost per child in a child care center accredited by the National Association for the Education of Young Children (NAEYC) to be approximately $4,900. This is in sharp contrast with what parents currently pay on average: $3,173 for center-based care and $2,565 for family child care. The GAO estimate of quality care does not, however, take into consideration any possible increase in staff compensation to reduce turnover. An analysis by Barbara Willer of NAEYC offers a new assessment of what it would cost to provide quality care if increases in caregiver salaries were taken into account. Willer suggests that the full cost of center-based care would range from $6,364 to $8,345 if salaries were improved substantially to lower turnover.[18] In a survey of the cost of care in Colorado, Culkin, Helburn, and Morris derived a similar estimate of nearly $8,300 for the full production cost of a nonprofit child care center for three- to five-year-olds. This calculation also assumes higher salaries and takes into account a variety of hidden subsidies, such as donated space and voluntary services.[19]

23

High-quality child care, then, is an expensive proposition for both individuals and society. On the one hand, many parents at low- to middle-income levels are unable or reluctant to pay the full cost of high-quality care, especially if there is more than one child in the family needing care. At the same time, however, it is unrealistic to expect that taxpayers will provide the very large subsidies necessary for all children to be enrolled in expensive programs. This tension between the competing goals of quality and affordability raises fundamental and difficult issues regarding the appropriate standards for quality and for the amounts and distribution of subsidies. It also raises the question of whether in some circumstances it may be more cost-effective for society to provide a greater incentive for one parent in a two-parent family to stay home rather than to subsidize child care, especially for the youngest children.

GOVERNMENT CHILD CARE PROGRAMS

Families at all income levels are likely to receive some kind of government subsidy, whether it takes the form of tax credits or

Figure 3

Federal Child Care Programs

PROGRAM	Child Care and Development Block Grant (CCDBG)	Social Services Block Grant (SSBG)	Dependent Care Tax Credit (DCTC)	Dependent Care Assistance Program (DCAP)
INCOME REQUIREMENTS	Family income less than 75% of state median income.	Open to state discretion.	No income limits, although percentage of expenses used to determine credit declines from 30% to 20% as income increases from $10,000 to $28,000.	No income limits.
ELIGIBILITY REQUIREMENTS	Qualified children are those under 13. Parents must be working or attending job training.	Open to state discretion.	Amount of credit decreases dollar per dollar for deduction in gross income under DCAP. Children must be under 13.	Employer must set up a flexible spending account for employees' child care. Children must be under 13.
PROGRAM TYPE	Capped federal entitlement. No state matching.	Capped federal entitlement. No state matching.	Nonrefundable credit against income tax liability.	Amounts paid by employers excluded from employee's gross taxable income.
REGULATORY REQUIREMENTS	Providers must meet all state and local standards; those exempted from such standards must be registered with state.	Open to state discretion.	Taxpayer must report name, address, and taxpayer ID of provider.	Taxpayer must report name, address, and taxpayer ID of provider.

incentives, vouchers, or direct monetary or in-kind subsidies to providers. However, the federal government's system of overlapping subsidies is highly fragmented and creates serious inefficiencies and inequities for families of different means.[20]

Financial assistance is provided primarily in two ways:

- Supply-side (or provider) subsidies that are designed to expand the number of child care spaces for low-income children

- Demand-side (or consumer) subsidies that provide parents with direct reimbursement for a portion of child care expenses and are meant to increase the choices of care available to parents

The number of federal programs that in some way affect child care has proliferated to an astounding degree. In a 1989 report, the GAO identified forty-six federal programs that provided some type of assistance in fiscal 1988. The Department of Labor details thirty-one programs in eleven federal agencies that support child care in some way.[21] Legislative activity since 1988 creating the Child Care and Development Block Grant and the Family Sup-

FSA Program: AFDC Child Care	FSA Program: Transitional Child Care (TCC)	At-Risk Child Care	Child Care Food Program	Head Start
Gross income less than 185% of state "need" level. Net income less than state payment standard (approximately equal to need standard).	No federal maximum income limit. State determines copayment based on family income.	No federal maximum income limit. State determines copayment based on family income.	No income test for nonprofit centers or family child care; in for-profit centers, at least 25% of children must receive support under the SSBG.	90% of children in program must be below poverty level. Higher-income children may participate with copayment, based on income.
AFDC eligible, assistance needed to accept employment, remain employed, or receive training. Transitional care available for first year off welfare rolls.	Must have received AFDC in 3 of previous 6 months. Must be leaving AFDC due to increased earnings, increased hours of work, or loss of income disregards.	Must be low-income family at risk of becoming eligible for welfare if child care assistance is not provided.	Federal reimbursement rates essentially the same as for the school lunch program: three-tiered subsidy levels, based on family income.	10% of spots reserved for children with disabilities. Federal authorization for children from birth to age five.
Open-ended state-matching federal entitlement.	Open-ended state-matching federal entitlement.	Capped state-matching federal entitlement.	Provides subsidy for meals and snacks served to children in child care.	Comprehensive preschool program. Grants are awarded by Department of Health and Human Services to public agencies, nonprofit organizations, and school systems.
Providers must meet all applicable state and local standards.	Providers must meet all applicable state and local standards.	Same as AFDC. Plus, providers exempted from state and local regulations must register with state.	None for nonprofit centers or family care homes; for-profit centers must enroll minimum percentage of children receiving state subsidies.	Various performance standards, as specified by the DHHS.

port Act have added to the number of initiatives. There are eight major federal programs (for a detailed description, see the Appendix).

- The **Dependent Care Tax Credit (DCTC)** provides working parents with a tax credit for child care expenses. Funding for this program has almost tripled in constant terms since it was first established in 1977. Its benefits go largely to middle- and upper-income families, primarily because it is not refundable.

- The **Social Services Block Grant (SSBG)** is used in part by most states to buy child care for low-income families, either by paying the provider directly or by giving parents a subsidy, often in the form of a voucher.

- The **Child Care and Development Block Grant (CCDBG)**, enacted in 1991, provides additional money to states to upgrade the supply and quality of child care for low-income children. The funds go directly to the states through a formula based on the number of children eligible for free or reduced-price school lunches.

- The **Dependent Care Assistance Program (DCAP)**, also known as the Dependent Care Exclusion, allows workers whose companies participate in the program to deduct up to $5,000 in pretax dollars for child care expenses. The DCAP primarily benefits middle- and upper-income families.

- The **Family Support Act (FSA)** provides federal funding to assist states in providing care for children of parents who take jobs or participate in education or training to prepare them for jobs. The FSA is really two programs: The first is for parents currently receiving AFDC; the second is transitional child care for the first year the parent is off the welfare rolls and in a paying job.

- **At-Risk Child Care** funds are available to states to assist parents who are now work-

ing but who might be in danger of sliding into welfare if they do not have help with child care costs.

- **Head Start** is, strictly speaking, not child care but a part-day compensatory education program for poor children. Although few Head Start programs are full day, some parents use the program as a form of child care, and it is the largest early childhood education program for low-income children.

- The **Child Care Food Program** provides nutritional assistance to caregivers serving needy children.

In addition to the programs that directly subsidize child care, the federal government has two income-supplement programs that low-income working parents can use to increase their disposable income and, presumably, the amount they spend on child care. These are the Earned Income Tax Credit and the Supplemental Newborn Tax Credit, both of which are refundable. The newborn tax credit, which is for dependent children under the age of one, cannot be used in conjunction with the DCTC; parents must choose one or the other. (These programs are described in more detail in the Appendix.)

According to the NRC, between 1972 and 1987, federal support for child care increased by 127 percent after inflation. A key question is whether the increase in federal subsidies has actually benefited those families that have the greatest financial need and the disadvantaged children who stand to benefit the most from better-quality care. Overall, those benefiting least from government child care subsidies are low- to moderate-income working families that earn more than the poverty level but less than $25,000 per year and those families that earn less than $15,000 a year but that do not have access to subsidized child care and pay up to one-quarter of their household income for care out of pocket.

Figure 4

Federal Programs Supporting Child Care-Related Services, 1990-1992

(in billions, all numbers approximate)

Program	Estimated Funding
Dependent Care Tax Credit	$4.000
Social Services Block Grant, Title XX	0.428[a]
Child Care and Development Block Grant	0.825
Head Start	2.200
Dependent Care Assistance Program	0.065
Family Support Act Child Care (AFDC & TCC)	0.429
At-Risk Child Care	0.383
Child Care Food Program	1.200
Total	$9.530

[a]The 30 states reporting usage of the SSBG spent approximately 15.3 percent of their grants on child care services. Total SSBG allocation in 1992 was $2.8 billion. However, since the 30 states may not be representative of all states, this figure is a rough approximation only.

SOURCE: Various government agencies.

The evidence would suggest that in terms of their ability to gain access to higher-quality center-based care, the poorest families benefit most from subsidies that go directly to providers to increase the number of child care slots.

The mix of supply-side and demand-side subsidies provided by the federal government has changed substantially in the past two decades; the result has been a dramatic decline in the percentage of federal child care resources benefiting low-income families. In 1972, 80 percent of federal child care dollars was targeted at low-income families through provider subsidies. In 1980, low-income families benefited from 50 percent of federal expenditures, primarily through the SSBG program and Head Start. By 1986, these programs accounted for only 26 to 30 percent of such expenditures.[22] The GAO documented a smaller but never theless significant shift from 83 percent of federal support going to low-income parents in 1977 to 54 percent in 1988.

By the early 1980s, then, direct consumer subsidies, primarily through the DCTC, had become the predominant form of federal support for child care.[23] The DCTC was originally intended to provide some financial relief to lower-income families who needed to pay for child care in order to work. In this tax credit's earliest incarnation in the 1960s, child care was viewed in part as an ordinary deductible business expense; but in reality, the benefits were limited to gainfully employed women, widowers, and divorced men with low incomes. Over the years, the tax credit has come to be viewed less as a business deduction and more as financial assistance for low-income families. Nevertheless, in recent years, the credit has been expanded to cover more families with higher incomes, to the point that it now delivers its greatest benefits to middle- and upper-income families with mothers who work outside the home. This is largely because many lower-income families have no tax liability, and the credit is not refundable.

The maximum credit is 30 percent of child care expenses for families earning less than $10,000. The maximum dollar value of the credit is $720, based on maximum claimable expenses of $2,400 for one child. The credit declines 1 percent for every $2,000 of income over $10,000 until at $28,000 it stabilizes at 20 percent for all higher incomes. Despite the higher allowable percentage for low-income families, the credit is worth virtually nothing to families earning under $10,000 a year and only $165 to families submitting joint returns earning $14,000 a year with one dependent.

In 1988, the DCTC accounted for nearly two-thirds of the funding for all federal programs supporting child care-related services.[24] According to the NCCS, the tax credit was used by 22 percent of families with employed mothers that had incomes under $15,000 and 29 percent of families with incomes under $25,000. In contrast, fully 37 percent of families with incomes over $50,000 used this source of subsidy.[25] Overall, 35 percent of families with employed mothers who have children under the age of five used this tax credit.

A smaller but increasingly significant federal contribution to child care is the DCAP, which treats child care expenses as a business deduction. This program allows employers to set up flexible spending accounts for employees through which they may deduct the pretax cost of child care from their income. Although the total amount of money going to families through the DCAP is small (only about $65 million in 1988), the program is fairly regressive. Because expenses are deducted from taxable income, this subsidy is worth more to those in higher tax brackets. For example, a family in the 31 percent federal tax bracket deducting the full $5,000 from taxable income would save $1,550 in taxes, plus additional tax savings from their state and/or local taxes, more than twice what a family earning $10,000 is theoretically eligible to receive as a maximum benefit under the DCTC.

Despite the regressive nature of the DCAP compared with the child care tax credit, the DCAP is often the first child care assistance program in which businesses participate. Aside from the paperwork and accounting involved, participating entails almost no costs for employers. Once companies become comfortable with this form of child care assistance, they often explore other ways of helping employees to meet their child care needs.

The financial contribution of state and local governments is generally quite small when compared with federal subsidies, totaling less than $500 million annually, according to the NRC. However, most of that money is concentrated in a few large states, such as California, which alone contributed $315 million in direct funds to a wide variety of child care programs in 1988. State involvement in child care is more significant in terms of setting standards and licensing procedures and in establishing part-day preschool programs.

The CCDBG program is too new to be assessed for its effect on the behavior of states in such areas as standards and licensing. The block grant requires that all providers who receive funding must be registered with the state, must comply with all applicable state and local laws, and must meet minimum health and safety standards.

A recent study for the Packard Foundation used data from the PCCS to examine the impact of various government policies on child care quality. The researchers concluded that the most influential impact on center quality was from direct government subsidies to programs that serve low-income children.[26] This conclusion supports the observations of the *National Child Care Staffing Study* (NCCSS), which found that the highest-quality centers were those that were government-subsidized to serve low-income children and those used by the highest-income families. The problem is that a much lower proportion of low-income children are enrolled in formal programs than children from middle- or high-income families.[27] The Packard Foundation study could find no independent impact on quality from tax credits. However, it found that the greatest variance in center quality was between wealthier and poorer states.[28]

One possible reason consumer subsidies do not appear to affect child care quality is that parents often do not connect the benefit they receive from the DCTC with their direct expenditures on child care. Rather, many view the tax credit as a mechanism for reducing their tax bill, instead of as additional income with which they could purchase higher-quality child care. This is partly because parents have to pay their child care provider on a weekly or monthly basis but do not see a benefit from the tax credit until the end of the year.

Another alternative to both tax credits and direct provider subsidies is child care vouchers. In fact, in response to both the CCDBG and a growing emphasis on parental choice, states are increasingly switching away from contracting child care services directly with providers in favor of greater reliance on vouchers.[29]

The advantages of vouchers are that parents have more leeway in choosing their provider and that the government is assured the money it allocates for child care is used for that purpose. However, by themselves, vouchers are not an effective tool for assuring that families receive quality child care. In many communities, particularly in low-income areas, no decent-quality child care programs exist; vouchers do not effectively increase parental choice if there are no alternatives from which to choose. In addition, many parents lack sufficent information with which to choose quality care.[30]

In communities where a variety of quality programs exist and parents have enough information to make good choices, vouchers can provide an effective method of consumer subsidy. However, where these criteria are not met (which may include most low-income neighborhoods), direct subsidies remain the most effective tool for guaranteeing the development of quality programs and ensuring parents access to these programs. In low-income communities, subsidies through contracts for child care slots may more effectively match families with quality services. Direct contracts ensure that providers will have a stable customer base and a regular income, which enables them to plan for personnel and facilities, thereby enhancing quality.[31]

We believe that in an era of limited resources and large budget deficits, federal funding for child care should be targeted to assist families with the greatest financial need and families whose children require special services. We see the need for a combined strategy of consumer and provider subsidies to accomplish this.

First, the dependent care tax credit should be made refundable in order to provide a larger relative benefit to families at the lower end of the income scale.* In addition, a mechanism should be explored to provide the credit at regular intervals so that parents will associate it more closely with child care costs. The additional cost of refundability could be made up by lowering the income level at which the DCTC and the Dependent Care Assistance Program phase out or by decreasing the benefit levels for higher-income families.

Second, we support the provision of direct government subsidies to programs that serve low-income children, since a number of studies show that such subsidies have the greatest impact on the quality of center-based care. However, more research needs to be done on the appropriate balance of these two approaches for improving child care quality and assisting parents in obtaining quality care that is affordable.

Third, we support a blended system of direct subsidies and vouchers tailored to the needs of individual communities. This combined approach can provide both stability and quality of services and increased parental choice, especially in low-income neighborhoods. Furthermore, as a way of tying public funding to quality programming, we recommend that both direct provider subsidies and vouchers be restricted to child care that meets state standards.

---

*See memorandum by OWEN B. BUTLER (page 68).

Chapter 4

STRATEGIES FOR IMPROVING THE QUALITY OF THE CHILD CARE SYSTEM

The key question involving child care quality is whether the additional costs of higher quality will be justified by its benefits for children, parents, business, and society at large. We believe that in the long term, substantially greater investment in child care will be justified but that the reality of limited resources in the near future will require especially difficult choices. We believe that the following areas are most important for public policy and private-sector involvement to address in both the near and the long term:

- The child care needs of low-income children and families

- The compensation and training of child care staff

- The quality of family child care homes

- The special care needs of infants and toddlers

- Health and safety and quality standards at the state and local levels to protect young children

- The importance of providing all parents with better information and assistance in finding quality child care

SERVING LOW-INCOME CHILDREN AND FAMILIES

Over the last few years, a patchwork of programs at the federal and state levels has been created specifically to serve low-income families, but there are serious gaps in coverage. Funds provided through the Social Services Block Grant (SSBG, Title XX), the Child Care and Development Block Grant (CCDBG), the Family Support Act (FSA), and the At-Risk Program have been directed to the child care needs of low-income parents, both those who are working and those who are trying to move off the welfare rolls. On the other hand, the tax-based subsidies, especially the dependent care tax credit (DCTC), which accounts for over 40 percent of all federal funds for child care, tend to benefit middle- and upper-income taxpayers to a greater degree, even though the original intent was to deliver a larger benefit to lower-income families.

There are two major changes required to improve the access of low-income families to better-quality care. The first (discussed in Chapter 3) is to realign tax-based subsidies so that lower-income families receive a higher monetary benefit and better-quality child care is made more affordable. The second is to improve the programs that serve low-income disadvantaged children. These programs should provide access to the comprehensive education, health, and social services most needed by these children and should conform more closely to the scheduling needs of working parents.

Although subsidies provided by the SSBG and the CCDBG have enabled some programs to deliver high-quality full-day care to low-income children, only a small percentage of such children actually receive quality care.

Giving the highest priority to quality improvements in programs for these children makes sense both as a matter of equity and because, as noted in Chapter 2, improvements in quality probably have the most impact on development when quality is low.

The NRC has noted that in 1981, SSBG programs served only 13 percent of eligible children; although the number of eligibles has grown since then, SSBG funding has actually declined by 55 percent in real terms.[1] Additional poor children are now being served by funds through the CCDBG and the FSA programs. The CCDBG is too new to have amassed data on how many children it serves; but based on funding levels for 1992, a rough estimate would be 250,000. The FSA child care programs serve about 211,000 on average. Head Start serves approximately 603,000 children, mostly ages three to five and mostly in part-day programs (see Figure 1).

However, because programs often try to combine funding sources to provide full-day services, there is probably considerable overlap in the actual children being served.

Clearly, the available information on exactly how many children in low-income families need full-day care and how many are currently receiving it is inadequate. For example, despite improved federal reporting requirements for the SSBG, many states do not provide this information, which makes it very difficult to find out exactly how many children are receiving care through the program. **We urge that the federal and state governments give high priority to improving data collection on child care and early childhood education. We also recommend that the reporting requirements for how states use federal child care funds be tightened, so that there are better data on how funds are being utilized.**

Figure 1

Estimates of Head Start Population and Percent Served, Fiscal 1992

Age	Population 1992 [a]	Economically Eligible for Head Start 1991 [b]	Eligibles, Not in Public Kindergarten	Enrolled in Head Start 1/92 [c]	Estimated Percent Served [d]
Under Age 3	11,825,000	3,439,000	3,439,000	18,632	1%
Age 3 to 5	11,381,000	2,999,000	2,116,900	602,445	29%
Age 3	3,859,000	1,066,000	1,066,000	167,691	16%
Age 4	3,785,000	979,000	979,000	391,279	40%
Age 5	3,738,000	954,000	286,900	43,475	16%

[a]Estimated population, based on Congressional Research Service (CRS) estimates from the March 1992 *Current Population Survey* (CPS).

[b]Estimates prepared by CRS from the March 1992 CPS. Based on the percentage of children living in families with income below the federal poverty income guidelines or living in families receiving AFDC in 1991.

[c]U.S. Department of Health and Human Services, Administration for Children, Youth and Families. According to DHHS, 95 percent of Head Start enrollees are eligible on the basis of their low-income status.

[d]Number of children participating in Head Start as a percentage of the economically eligible population not in public kindergarten. Participation rates assume that 30 percent of eligible five-year-olds are not enrolled in public kindergarten and are therefore candidates for Head Start.

SOURCE: Table prepared by Congressional Research Service.

MEETING THE COMPREHENSIVE CARE AND EDUCATION NEEDS OF DISADVANTAGED CHILDREN

In their first five years, disadvantaged children are most in need of an environment that addresses both their developmental and their educational needs because they are less likely than middle-class children to get adequate nurturing at home. Policy makers are trying to address this issue by expanding the Head Start program and creating preschool programs for the disadvantaged at the state level. However, these programs still enroll only a minority of eligible children, and the vast majority of Head Start programs and other preschools for the disadvantaged offer only part-day and part-year care. Head Start was not designed with working parents in mind and therefore does not meet the full-day care needs of low-income parents who are trying to work, finish school, or move from welfare to paid employment.

The FSA programs were designed specifically to provide child care to parents on public assistance who receive education and training or who take jobs. Unfortunately, the child care provisions of the act do not take into account the need that children from disadvantaged families have for comprehensive care that addresses their developmental and educational needs, such as that provided part time in good Head Start programs.

The federal government needs to allow states and local communities to coordinate the variety of child care and education options for poor children, including Head Start, FSA programs, and funding through the various block grant programs, so that families can use a single program that both provides full-day care and meets the developmental needs of their children.

WHOM DOES HEAD START SERVE?

Head Start is by far the most important and extensive early childhood education program designed to improve the school readiness of disadvantaged children. But even with substantial recent increases in funding and Congressional authorization of full funding by 1994, in 1991 Head Start still served only 29 percent of the total eligible population of three- to four-year-olds and those five-year-olds not already in kindergarten (see Figure 1). The recent priority has been to increase the number of slots for four-year-olds, of whom 40 percent are now enrolled; however, only 16 percent of eligible three-year-olds are participating in Head Start.

Figure 2

Cost of Head Start Full Funding Under Phase-in Plan

(dollars in billions)

FY	1991	1992	1993	1994	1995	1996
Percent Served	25%	40%	55%	70%	85%	100%
Age 3	$0.6	$1.0	$1.5	$2.0	$2.4	$2.9
Age 4	0.6	1.0	1.4	1.9	2.4	2.9
Age 5	0.7	1.1	1.6	2.0	2.6	3.1
Total Cost	$1.9	$3. 1	$4.5	$5.9	$7.4	$8.9

SOURCE: U.S. Congressional Budget Office, Memorandum to Honorable Patricia Schroeder, Chairwoman, House Select Committee on Children, Youth and Families, July 30, 1991.

Therefore, Head Start still fails to reach more than two-thirds of the children who are eligible. A large proportion of children who might benefit from a comprehensive program such as Head Start are, instead, in child care arrangements that may not address their developmental needs. This is particularly true for children whose mothers are involved in education or work under the FSA requirements.

CED continues its strong support for universal access to comprehensive early intervention programs, such as Head Start, for disadvantaged children. However, we are concerned that many Head Start programs and other preschool programs implemented at the state level in the past few years are not meeting the real needs of the target population of children or their families for three key reasons: The quality of Head Start programs is uneven, they do not address the child care needs of many parents who work, and they exclude children younger than three or four who need access to comprehensive health, social, and educational services.

CHILD CARE UNDER
THE FAMILY SUPPORT ACT

Full implementation of the FSA is further complicating efforts to provide quality early care and education to disadvantaged children. Over two-thirds of the children who are eligible for Head Start come from families receiving AFDC. This is the same population of parents, mostly single mothers, who are expected to participate in FSA-required education and work programs; yet, the linkages between FSA-supported child care and Head Start are tenuous.

The FSA requires states to provide child care during the first year of training or employment and extended child care benefits for the first year that participants are employed and off the welfare rolls.[2] However, full implementation of the act may have several unintended effects. In some states, children from low-income families who are currently enrolled in subsidized care centers may be displaced by children whose mothers are in the FSA program. In addition, children involved in FSA child care would be eligible for Head Start, but this may not be an option for many FSA families. Because 90 percent of Head Start programs offer only part-day care, some FSA mothers may be forced to remove their children from Head Start to place them in all-day care settings that do not provide similar educational, health, and social services. Furthermore, the federal FSA regulations have the effect of limiting the ability of states to set standards for eligible child care on the grounds that standards which are too high could exclude some categories of care and limit parental choice. Yet, parents in the FSA programs have little assistance available to help them make choices and determine the most appropriate care for their children.[3]

Two recent studies indicate that because of deficiencies in federal and state implementation of the FSA, a majority of eligible families are getting either no child care benefits or care of substandard quality. The delivery gap is widest for the transitional child care that is supposed to be available during the first year the mother is in the paid labor force. Both studies found that lack of information and inefficient administration of the program are responsible in most cases for this situation.[4]

THE NEED FOR MORE
FULL-DAY COMPREHENSIVE
CHILD CARE PROGRAMS

Many disadvantaged children who could be benefiting from the kind of comprehensive care, education, and health services offered by Head Start are not receiving them because few full-day child care settings provide such services. This is particularly true for infants and toddlers; for example, only 1 percent of children in this age group who are economically eligible for Head Start have access to comprehensive services through the program's parent-child centers, which is only a part-time program. Few full-day child care settings offer the comprehensive services Head Start would provide.

Policy makers should explore a variety of ways to improve the access of low-income families, particularly those with infants and toddlers, to full-day child care that provides needed services similar to those offered by Head Start. This could be accomplished through such mechanisms as providing parents with vouchers for centers or licensed family care homes or allowing Head Start programs to serve younger children. Nevertheless, for three- to five-year-olds, Head Start does provide an important child development infrastructure on which to build expanded services that can meet the needs of both low-income children and parents more effectively.

The overwhelming majority of Head Start programs as well as other state-sponsored preschool programs provide only part-day and part-year care. This limits access for the children of the working poor who need full-day care. If they want their children to participate in Head Start, these parents have to make complicated multiple arrangements to accommodate their full-time working schedules.

Ironically, a Head Start enrollment and recruitment study indicated that the desirability of enrolling their children can serve as a disincentive to employment for parents. Although 40 percent of the parents with children on the Head Start waiting list were employed, only 28.5 percent of the parents of enrolled children were employed. The need to work and use full-day care can also prevent many parents from enrolling children who would otherwise benefit from the program. According to the same study, this was the second most frequent reason for families taking their children out of Head Start.[5]

Providing more full-day Head Start services will be essential for meeting the needs of welfare-dependent or at-risk parents and children. A 1990 study by the GAO estimates the average cost of a full-day, high-quality early childhood program that meets the accreditation standards of the National Association for the Education of Young Children (NAEYC) to be approximately $4,900 per child. The National Head Start Association estimates that with the more comprehensive health, education, and social services Head Start offers, it would require approximately $5,400 per child to deliver improved-quality programs to all children currently enrolled as well as provide full-day and full-year services to 25 percent of the children. Since states are required to provide a 20 percent match in funds, the federal contribution would be $4,320. In contrast, the actual 1991 federal Head Start expenditure was $3,159 per child.[6] There are approximately 2.1 million children between the ages of three and five who are economically eligible for Head Start and not otherwise enrolled in kindergarten. It would cost approximately $6.6 billion to enroll them all in the current part-day Head Start program and $9.0 billion to enroll them in an improved-quality program that provides 25 percent of the children with full-day, full-year services. This could allow a substantial number of eligible children whose parents work full time or who are participating in FSA job and training programs to participate in Head Start. Figure 2 lists the estimates developed by the Congressional Budget Office to enroll all eligible three- to five-year-old children in Head Start's current program by 1996.

IMPROVING AND EXPANDING HEAD START

Expansion of Head Start should not occur without corresponding improvements in the overall quality of its programs. Enrollment policies that place priority on four-year-olds ignore the fact that by the time they are that old, many poor children already have severe language and social skill problems.

The quality of both Head Start and state-sponsored preschools can vary considerably from program to program.[7] The Head Start Expansion and Quality Improvement Act of 1990 authorized that 25 percent of the increased funds for 1993 be spent on improving program quality. Nonetheless, the Administration proposed at the time that only

7 percent of this money be used to address the quality issue; the rest of the increase was to be used to expand the program for four-year-olds.[8]

We are concerned that if expansion proceeds without improving the quality of the program, Head Start will fail to realize its potential. Policy makers are beginning to recognize the need for expansion and quality to go hand in hand. The Head Start Expansion and Quality Improvement Act mandated that at least half of the $194 million appropriated for quality improvements in 1991 be designated for salary increases, and programs were given the discretion to use virtually all the funds for that purpose.[9]

Another important quality improvement would be to upgrade the management skills of Head Start directors, who often must cobble together a variety of funding sources and coordinate programs in order to meet the increasingly complex care needs of the children. A number of creative efforts are cur-

rently under way to address this issue. One of the most encouraging is the effort recently established by Johnson & Johnson to help directors cope with the rapid expansion of the program while maintaining and upgrading its quality.

Rapid Head Start expansion will also have to deal with a serious lack of facilities. Many programs are housed in substandard buildings or have lost space previously donated by or rented from community groups or schools. The National Head Start Association estimates that taxpayers "lost" nearly $13 million on renovations of now-vacated facilities between 1987 and 1990.[10] Until 1992, Head Start programs were enjoined by law from owning their own facilities. Although the law was recently changed, programs still face a dearth of affordable space that is suitable for young children. At least one innovative partnership in New Jersey, jointly sponsored by the Prudential Foundation and Invest in Children, a

JOHNSON & JOHNSON HEAD START MANAGEMENT FELLOWS PROGRAM

To help Head Start directors cope with the rapid expansion of the program because of increased government funding and equip them with the management skills that will help them address the shortcomings of the program as it currently exists, Johnson & Johnson established a new Management Fellows Program. The program provides local Head Start directors with management training at the John E. Anderson Graduate School of Management at the University of California at Los Angeles. Funded by a three-year, $1.2 million grant from the company, the program was developed in response to a Johnson & Johnson-commissioned study that indicated that Head Start directors would benefit from advanced management skills training. The grant covers the development of the program, tuition, special events, and other academic costs.

During each year of the program, forty local Head Start directors are chosen to partici-

pate in a two-week course at UCLA to sharpen their skills in strategic planning, developing and managing financial and human resources, and program evaluation. Participating directors are required to develop a Management Improvement Project to be undertaken in the following year to enhance their Head Start programs back home.

The program has already left its mark on many Head Start programs throughout the country. For example, Head Start directors in Mississippi (Holly Springs), Rhode Island (Newport), North Carolina (Franklin), and Florida (Winterhaven) have already made significant changes to their programs that have led to improved and expanded services for their communities. They have also provided management training to other staff members, thereby extending the benefits of the Johnson & Johnson Management Fellows Program.

SOURCE: Johnson & Johnson Head Start Management Program

coalition of New Jersey business, education, human services, and advocacy groups, is attempting to solve this problem.

As we noted in Chapter 2, Head Start children also benefit from better continuity between their preschool and elementary schooling. Recent research shows that the intellectual gains made during Head Start eventually fade unless there is considerable follow-through well into the elementary school years. Several limited projects have attempted to provide such follow-through, but none has gone beyond the pilot stage. A promising new program, implemented in 1991, is the Head Start Transition Project. Designed to serve Head Start children from kindergarten through third grade, it is the first follow-up effort to include the same range of comprehensive

health, education, parental involvement, and social services as the Head Start program itself. Because it is so new, it will not be possible to evaluate the program's effectiveness for quite some time.

The federal government has also established a project to encourage Head Start programs and states to work together more effectively. Head Start has always required that states provide a 20 percent match in funding (and a number of states provide considerably more), but historically, there has been little state involvement in Head Start or coordination of Head Start and state-run preschool programs. The purpose of the new collaborative project is to "create significant, statewide partnerships between Head Start and the states in order to meet the increasingly complex and difficult

---

EARLY CHILDHOOD FACILITIES FUND FOR NEW JERSEY

Invest in Children, a coalition of New Jersey's business, education, human services, and advocacy groups, established the Early Childhood Facilities Fund (ECFF) to help the state increase the number and quality of Head Start sites. The fund was created as a result of a study funded by a $75,000 grant from the Prudential Foundation. The study revealed that because of inadequate facilities for Head Start programs, the state was unprepared to expand and improve Head Start enrollments in response to increased federal funding. According to the study, Head Start programs are plagued by a number of problems that include "substandard conditions, insecure and short-term leases, inadequate space, inefficiency of multiple sites, and inadequate outdoor play areas." A national survey ranked New Jersey among the bottom ten states for the condition of its facilities.

Head Start in New Jersey currently serves 11,688 children ages three to five, about 35 percent of the estimated 33,160 children ages three to five with family incomes below the poverty level. With additional federal dollars

now available to expand and improve Head Start (about $5 to $6 million for New Jersey), new facilities need to be constructed and others renovated to accommodate the expansion. According to Peter Goldberg, president of the Prudential Foundation, "Having child-friendly spaces is an aspect of the Head Start program that people just haven't paid attention to. This can be a very important step forward for New Jersey in fulfilling its commitment to making sure all children coming to school are ready to learn."

The fund expects to raise $5 million from corporate and philanthropic sources over the next three years. The New Jersey Department of Human Services has already pledged a $150,000 start-up grant, and the Prudential Foundation will provide $600,000 for the first three-year period. Over the next three years, the fund plans to finance nine new or substantially rehabilitated Head Start centers, to assess the facility needs of thirty early childhood programs, and to finance the renovation of thirty-nine Head Start centers and child care facilities. ECFF will be incorporated as a private, non-profit, tax-exempt organization.

SOURCE: Invest in Children and the Prudential Foundation

challenges of improving services for low-income children and their families." Twenty-two states are currently receiving funding to participate.

We make a number of recommendations for improving the early care and education of disadvantaged children. First, Head Start programs should enroll approximately as many three-year-olds as four-year-olds.

Second, we believe that upgrading the quality of Head Start is as important as expanding access to the program if lasting results are to be obtained, and we would support expanding enrollment at a slower pace so that additional funding can be earmarked to upgrade quality, improve salaries, and expand full-day services. Phased-in full-funding targets for Head Start, which were authorized by Congress in 1991, should be revised to reflect the need to upgrade Head Start quality so that funding will be adequate eventually to meet the needs of all eligible three- and four-year-olds, as well as five-year-olds not otherwise in kindergarten, in good-quality programs.

Third, strong linkages between Head Start programs, FSA-approved child care options, and full-day services for other low-income children should be developed. Some of the increases in Head Start funding should be used to expand the number of full-day programs that meet the dual need for child care and intensive early childhood education for children of working parents or those who are participating in the FSA program. Head Start rules requiring parental participation in the program should be revised to allow more children of parents who are employed full time to stay in the program. Funding sources should be able to be combined more easily so that more Head Start and other comprehensive preschool programs would be able to provide full-day care for children of working parents at a single site.

Fourth, because sustained intervention is critical for maintaining the learning gains preschoolers make in Head Start, we believe that every effort should be made to provide follow-through in elementary school for Head Start graduates and other disadvantaged children.

Fifth, we recommend an expansion of the Head Start parent-child centers and similar family support programs to serve the comprehensive care needs of disadvantaged children from birth through age three.

Sixth, whether or not they are enrolled in Head Start, for poor and other disadvantaged children whose parents work or are in school, it is essential that child care be linked in some way to a variety of family support services, such as parent education and support, family literacy, and health care.

UPGRADING THE QUALITY OF CHILD CARE STAFF

If the successful development of children in child care is largely determined by the quality of the relationship with the caregiver, the staffing of care centers and family care homes must be a central policy concern. Because personnel costs account for the bulk of the operating expenses of child care centers, changes in staff-child ratios or salaries will significantly affect the cost of care.

Better outcomes for children are related both to the training of the caregiver and to the stability of the child-caregiver relationship. Training in child development promotes more appropriate interactions between caregiver and child that, in turn, contribute to the child's language and cognitive development. Although good data on the level of caregiver training are difficult to come by, particularly for those who work in nonregulated family child care, the most recent evidence suggests that education and training levels have been increasing in both center care and family child care.[11]

Although stability of relationships is extremely important, turnover among child care workers tends to be very high. Average annual turnover for teachers in all child care programs is 25 percent, but this varies from

14 percent in public-school-sponsored programs to 39 percent among for-profit child care chains.[12]

Low salaries, lack of benefits, and the absence of a clear career path are often cited as leading factors in this high turnover. In 1988, a study of five cities found that the average hourly wage for all staff members in child care centers was $5.35, which amounts to $9,363 per year. Forty-two percent of child care teachers, assistant teachers, and aides earned at least half of their household income, and one-quarter earned over two-thirds of it. Fully 25 percent of full-time staff found it necessary to work a second job.[13]

Salaries vary considerably in the different types of child care programs. A 1990 national survey found that the average annual salary of a preschool teacher in a child care center was $11,500; the median salary was $11,000. Teachers in full-day programs earned an average of $6.84 an hour, $5.43 an hour in for-profit programs and $14.40 in public-school-based programs.[14] Child care staff generally receive few employment benefits. Although 48 percent of all U.S. workers have disability coverage, few or no child care workers have this benefit. Only one-third to one-half of child care workers have any kind of employer health coverage. Other benefits, such as pensions and life insurance, are received by perhaps one-quarter of child care employees.[15]

We believe that strategies should be developed at the federal and state levels to improve the compensation and training of child care teachers and other child care workers with the express goal of reducing the high turnover among staff.

PROMOTING QUALITY IN FAMILY CHILD CARE

Most studies of child care quality have been conducted in center-based settings, and their findings are difficult to generalize to family child care. In terms of such characteristics as child-to-staff ratio and group size, family care measures up well. However, in terms of the quality of interaction between caregiver and child, the structure and content of children's activities, and the stability of the caregiver relationship, family care quality is unpredictable at best.

Virtually all child care centers are licensed and therefore under some public scrutiny, but only about 10 to 18 percent of family care homes are.[16] The *National Day Care Home Study* (NDCHS) found that in those family care homes that are regulated, the interactions between caregivers and children are of higher quality. The NDCHS also found that those regulated homes that are "sponsored" (i.e., in some kind of network association) tended to provide the highest levels of caregiver interactions with children and that unregulated homes had the lowest.[17] It is unclear, however, how much these differences were due to a self-selection bias, with better providers choosing to be regulated or to join a network.

Unlike staff in child care centers, family care providers tend to be isolated, with few opportunities to share tasks, interact with colleagues, or find other forms of adult support. Participation in a family care network and the availability of periodic supervision would alleviate this isolation, would provide professional support and educational resources, and could significantly improve the quality of daily experiences for the children.[18]

In France, family day care networks (*crèches familiales*) are organized into hubs that link from six to as many as thirty-five homes. Each network is directed by a specially trained pediatric nurse who coordinates administration, training, activities, and equipment lending. The nurse-director hires and trains child care providers, matches each one with two or three children, supervises their training by specially qualified staff, maintains contact with municipal officials, and even organizes backup services for children whose providers get sick. The hub staff organizes small group sessions for caregivers and children during which caregivers can obtain training, information, or social support while children participate in educational activities.[19]

Another way to provide training opportunities and learning materials to family child care operators is to bring the resources and expertise directly to them. In Dade County, Florida, a partnership that includes the county, local Kiwanis Clubs, the National Council of Jewish Women, Greater Miami Section, and others sends the Resourcemobile, staffed by an early childhood educator and stocked with books, toys, and art materials, to family child care homes.

We believe that it is critically important to find creative ways to upgrade the quality of neighborhood-based family child care without increasing costs too greatly and reducing supply. This can be done in a number of ways, including expanding and improving resource and referral agencies and encouraging the development of networks of family care homes, which can offer providers greater access to a variety of educational resources, training opportunities, and professional interaction.

INFANT CARE AND PARENTAL LEAVE

Infant care is the area of fastest demand growth. More than half of all mothers with children under the age of one are now in the work force, and approximately one-third of these infants are in out-of-home care. The other two-thirds are being cared for by their parents (usually through shift work), by other relatives, or by nonrelated paid help. Nearly 60 percent of the infants in out-of-home care are in family child care homes, and 40 percent are in centers. Almost all family care homes seem to be willing to take very young children, compared with only

---

DADE COUNTY RESOURCEMOBILE FOR FAMILY CARE PROVIDERS

In an effort to provide training and support services to family care providers serving disadvantaged children in Dade County, public and private groups worked together to raise funds to start the Resourcemobile. The initial partners involved were the Kiwanis Clubs of Dade County, the National Council of Jewish Women, Greater Miami Section, the Junior League of Miami, and Metro Dade's Department of Human Resources. Currently, board members include representatives from Kiwanis, Dade County, Miami Dade Community College, Head Start, the Florida Association for Women Lawyers, and members of the community at large. The board sets the curriculum and policy for the project, and the county maintains the van and employs the staff, consisting of an early childhood educator and a driver.

The Resourcemobile is a fully equipped mobile unit that is stocked with the latest developmentally appropriate equipment, including art, toys, games, and books. The Resourcemobile operates Monday through Friday, from 8:00 A.M. to 5:00 P.M., and visits each family home approximately once every four weeks (after the initial visit), for thirty minutes to one hour, depending on the needs of the provider. The county early childhood educator conducts a brief developmentally appropriate learning activity with the children and works with providers to tailor a program to their needs. Providers receive free educational materials to enhance their curriculums. About forty family care providers are served monthly. In addition to the Resourcemobile, the partnership publishes a newsletter for family day care providers and holds training seminars two Saturdays per month to improve skills. With the help of the Resourcemobile, the family care providers recently formed an organization to enhance their professional development.

According to Rachel S. Blechman, president of Resourcemobile, "the project has been extremely successful." Her only regret is they would like to serve more providers, but their capacity is limited.

SOURCE: Dade County Kiwanis Clubs

half of all centers. Few nonemployed mothers use supplemental out-of-home care for their infants.[20]

The debate over the best way of addressing the child care needs of infants generally focuses on two issues: improving the availability of affordable, quality out-of-home infant care and providing more opportunities for new parents to take extended leave from work during their child's infancy.

SPECIAL CARE NEEDS OF INFANTS

Infants require special care that relates to their physical needs and health concerns. Because an infant's immune system takes time to mature, exposure to disease should be as limited as possible, and innoculations for common childhood diseases should be given as soon as advisable. Physical development takes place very rapidly during infancy, and babies need room to move about and a safe, protected environment to explore. Cognitive development also occurs rapidly, leading to the rudiments of language acquisition. Child development experts stress that babies need caregivers who are "tuned in" to their physical, cognitive, and emotional needs. Most important, infants and toddlers are completely dependent on their adult caregivers to meet their basic physical needs; they cannot tell their caregivers when to feed them, change them, or comfort them.[21]

IMPACT OF OUT-OF-HOME CARE ON INFANTS

The research literature on the effects of nonparental care on infants provides mixed and controversial conclusions. Some researchers, such as Jay Belsky, have held that more than twenty hours a week of nonparental care in infancy may be detrimental to later social and emotional development.[22] However, based on Swedish studies of quality care, Belsky has more recently come to believe that the quality of care makes a difference in how well infants fare. A host of newer studies by Alison Clarke-Stewart and others argue that in many

ways, infants who have been in good-quality care are more competent and emotionally resourceful.[23] However, other research appears to support concerns that maternal employment during the child's first year of life may have negative developmental effects on some nonpoor children, although this research fails to distinguish between infants in good-quality versus poor-quality settings.[24]

A recent study by researchers at the University of Wisconsin and University of Texas found that for low-income, single-mother families, maternal employment during infancy and the toddler years may even enhance children's intellectual development.[25] The researchers found that children who were in good-quality out-of-home care during their first three years while their mothers worked had higher math scores in the second grade than those reared at home. Other studies have also found higher math scores for children who had attended high-quality infant care than for those who did not begin child care until later.[26] Given the fact that *A Profile of Child Care Settings* (PCCS) and the *National Child Care Staffing Study* (NCCSS) both found that infants tend to be in poorer-quality programs than older children, there is reason for concern. **When out-of-home infant care is necessary, it should enhance the child's development during the critical first year and protect its health and safety.**

HIGH COST OF INFANT CARE

Whatever impact nonparental care may have on young infants, one of the most important drawbacks of such care is its substantially higher cost. All forms of child care are highly labor-intensive, and none more so than infant care. For both developmental and safety reasons, most experts agree that one caregiver should care for no more than three or four infants at a time.

It has been estimated that full-time infant care generally costs about one-third more than care for older preschoolers.[27] In Boston, for example, center-based care for a preschooler costs an average of $150 a week, but similar infant care costs $200.[28] This is clearly unaffordable for most low- and moderate-income parents, who are more likely to utilize less formal arrangements, which may or may not be of sufficient quality. Many two-parent families depend on arranging split shifts at work so that no supplemental care arrangements will be needed. Although parents often do this not only to reduce costs but also because they believe it is in the best interest of their children, at least one study has shown that such an arrangement often puts irreparable strain on the marriage.[29] Clearly, this would not, in the long run, be in the best interest of the children.

Single parents who represent the only family paycheck generally do not have the option of either arranging shift work or taking an unpaid leave of absence. Financial pressures dictate that many parents who would rather take time at home with their infants must work.

Most studies of child care availability indicate that even when other forms of care are plentiful in the market, good-quality infant care is scarce. Because of the high cost, there are no easy solutions for closing this gap. Nevertheless, we urge policy makers in collaboration with parents and child care providers to seek new strategies for making quality infant care more available and affordable.

PARENTAL LEAVE

Many child development experts question the wisdom of placing newborns in full-time out-of-home care before parents and other family members have had time to fully bond with their new child. Pediatrician T. Berry Brazelton considers a minimum of three to four months to be necessary for such bonding to take place. The Yale University Bush Center Advisory Committee on Infant Care Leave believes one year is ideal.

Business and government are increasingly recognizing the dilemma faced by new parents. A number of major corporations have crafted progressive family leave policies that allow parents to take time off, either paid or unpaid, for a specified period after the birth or adoption of a child. One of the most generous leave policies is offered by IBM. New parents may take up to one year of paid leave and up to two additional years of unpaid leave during which they must be available for part-time work. Health benefits are maintained during the entire leave period.

Although large and medium-size firms tend to make leave available either through disability insurance or through paid sick leave, a substantial majority of employees in small, medium-size, and large firms have no leave time available for infant care per se.[30] Companies are increasingly including fathers in their leave policies, but it is rare that a father will avail himself of this opportunity. A 1986 study by Catalyst found that 37 percent of companies in a sample of 384 offered unpaid leave to fathers, but only 9 companies reported fathers taking advantage of the policy.

More than half of the states have established policies on family leave. As of early 1992, twenty-eight states and the District of Columbia had passed laws requiring some type of leave covering private-sector or state employees or both.[31] According to one survey, twenty-seven states provide employees with benefit protection during leave, and twenty-three had some form of job protection. The survey found that extended leave was at the discretion of supervisors. Similarly, federal employees may use annual or sick leave for pregnancy and postpartum recovery at the discretion of supervisors.[32]

In February 1993, the federal government established a national family leave policy by enacting the Family and Medical Leave Act. This act requires companies with more than fifty employees to allow up to twelve weeks of unpaid leave for the birth or adoption of a child or to care for a child, parent, spouse, or oneself during a serious illness. It requires companies to maintain health benefits during the leave and to reinstate the employee to his or her previous job or an equivalent position upon return. Employees whose earnings are in the top 10 percent and whose leave would cause serious harm to the employer are exempted. Because of the exemption of small business, the Family and Medical Leave Act covers only 39 percent of the total work force.

Costs and Benefits of Parental Leave. There has been extensive discussion of the costs of mandated parental leave. Critics maintain that such leaves impose significant costs on employers, resulting in reduced employment, higher costs to consumers, lower wages, and discrimination against women of childbearing age. On the other hand, proponents argue that by increasing the attachment of workers to their employers, such leaves induce efficiency and thereby improve productivity. Research suggests that costs for paid parental leave, as found in most European countries, would be substantial. A study by Meryl Frank looked at the costs of a number of extensive family leave options. These costs (in 1988 dollars) ranged from $1.725 billion per year for a three-month leave with 50 percent salary replacement to slightly more than $7 billion for a six-month leave with 100 percent replacement.[33]

The net aggregate cost to business of a mandated unpaid family leave policy remains unclear. The GAO looked at the likely result of a twelve-week unpaid leave program, similar to that recently enacted, that would continue health benefits for parents with newborn or newly adopted children in firms with more than fifty workers. The GAO estimated that this mandated proposal would cover 39 percent of the total work force and about 5 percent of all U.S. firms. A little less than 40 percent of the 2.2 million working women who give birth each year would be covered by the proposal. The GAO found there would be little measurable net cost to employers associated with replacing workers or maintaining output while workers are on unpaid leave. It found that the cost to employers, primarily the cost of continuation of health insurance coverage, would be about $244 million annually (in 1992 dollars). When the other provisions of the legislation were included (medical leave to care for a seriously ill child, parent, spouse, or oneself), the total rose to $674 million. The actual

cost of these provisions is likely to be less, however, because they assume all eligible workers take the maximum leave available.[34]

Other studies focus on the economic benefits of parental leave deriving from the increased attachment of women to the labor force and increased labor force stability. Such social benefits may be reflected in substantial savings to business or in higher pay to workers. For instance, other researchers contend that the provision of unpaid leave results in substantial saving to business. Unlike the GAO, Eileen Trzcinsky and William T. Alpert estimated the saving to employers for providing unpaid leave from reduced turnover costs. They found that termination rates on account of illness and disability (including pregnancy and childbirth-related disabilities) were 49 percent lower for nonmanagers and nearly 94 percent lower for managers in businesses that provide job-guaranteed unpaid medical leave than in businesses that do not. Because of the high cost of replacing workers, they determined that businesses would incur a total saving of $719 million if job-guaranteed unpaid medical leave were available in all businesses with over fifty employees.[35]

Although a mandated family leave policy appears to result in few net costs to larger businesses in the aggregate, there is evidence that some individual firms may have difficulty complying. A three-year study by the Families and Work Institute of four states — Minnesota, Oregon, Rhode Island, and Wisconsin — which provide a range of parental leave policies found that half of employers said it was either "extremely easy" or "moderately easy" to comply with mandated leave. Nearly 40 percent found it "neither easy nor difficult" to comply, and another 9 percent found it "difficult" to comply.[36] We are particularly concerned about those individual firms that have substantial difficulty providing leave. In particular, small firms with little flexibility in personnel arrangements and industries that employ a large number of women are most vulnerable. In general, the research is inadequate to estimate the effect of a mandated leave policy on these companies.

The lack of parental leave, of course, imposes costs on the women who temporarily or permanently leave jobs for childbearing. For instance, a recent study estimated that the total earnings loss for women who bear children and return to work within two years is $12.9 billion annually. Those with access to leave sacrifice 51 percent of their prebirth annual earnings, and those without leave lose 86 percent. Furthermore, taxpayers may pay an additional $108 million in public assistance for these women.[37] However, these costs, even if undesirable, are largely transfers of income among members of society rather than costs to society as a whole.

There are also less tangible longer-term benefits of parental leave, however, such as stronger families and better developmental consequences for children,[38] which accrue to society at large rather than to current workers or businesses. Given the uncertainty about the effects of nonmaternal infant care, the special importance to infants of high-quality care, and the much higher costs of caring for infants compared with older children, parental leave appears a socially cost-effective alternative to out-of-home infant care for families who find this feasible. In fact, given the societal interest in such care, a strong argument can be made for flexibly subsidizing parental leave, for instance through a tax credit such as that proposed by the former Administration, in cases where such incentives are not outweighed by the burdens to firms and workers.

Although we endorse the principle of family leave, we are concerned that the costs of federally mandated leave have not been adequately studied. We are particularly concerned that a national policy of mandated leave for smaller firms would entail burdensome costs that would undermine their competitiveness and reduce employment. In lieu of extending mandates, we would favor tax-based incentives to encourage companies to provide leave to parents upon the birth or adoption of an infant. Despite these reserva- **tions, we believe that family-friendly workplace policies are in the best long-term interests of both employers and employees. We encourage companies of all sizes to develop flexible leave policies that would provide new parents with job protection and maintenance of health benefits for three to twelve months after childbirth. We also urge employers to implement other family-friendly policies, such as providing more part-time work with benefits, job sharing, flexible scheduling, and telecommuting to help parents more effectively balance the needs of work and family.**

GOVERNING CHILD CARE AND EARLY CHILDHOOD EDUCATION

There is little consistency in how child care and early childhood education programs are governed at the federal, state, and local levels. The 1990 legislation creating the CCDBG formalized state authority for determining standards and regulating child care. However, the federal government still regulates Head Start, which is a federal program.

In a few communities, child care and preschool are coordinated by or with the public school authorities. California has become the first state to establish a cabinet-level department that will attempt to oversee all policies affecting the welfare of children. For administrative purposes, all early childhood and child care services in California are now housed in the Child Development Division of the Department of Education. This has made it possible to combine funds for many programs and has improved coordination of services, assisted in establishing uniform quality standards, and provided opportunities for trying out innovative ideas.[39] Similar efforts are being undertaken in Maryland and West Virginia.

Success By 6, which began in Minneapolis and is now being replicated in more than two dozen cities around the country, is attempting to coordinate child care and early childhood programs at the local level. The city of Minneapolis also has long had a deputy mayor for youth services who helps the mayor focus on the needs of children and young people. The governor of Minnesota recently proposed a new agency that would combine all state programs for children from infancy through postsecondary education. However, few communities have true coordinating mechanisms and, therefore, little possibility for developing coherent programs and policies or accountability for program operation.

We believe that there should be a clear assignment of responsibilities for child care policy at the federal, state, and local levels of government. A high priority should be placed on reducing the number of overlapping child care programs and developing an administrative mechanism at each level to ensure that child care, early childhood education, and other policies and programs that affect children are effectively coordinated, integrated where possible, and made accessible to those who need them.

CHILD CARE STANDARDS AND REGULATION

The creation and enforcement of standards for child care programs is highly controversial. It is difficult for policy makers to resolve the conflict between the desire to improve the quality of out-of-home care and the fear that regulation will restrict the market.[40] Some analysts argue that uniform federal regulation or state regulations that specify improved ratios, group sizes, increased training, or credentials for staff could price some small providers out of the market, reduce the supply of affordable care, and raise costs for both parents and the public.[41] However, others maintain that it is possible to develop standards and regulations at the state and local levels that are not too costly or intrusive and that safeguard both health and safety and promote quality without adversely affecting the availability of services.[42]

Over the years, numerous attempts have been made to promulgate child care standards at the federal level; but with the exception of the short-lived Federal Interagency Day Care Requirements, which were terminated in 1982, the responsibility for establishing and enforcing standards has been left to the individual states and localities.[43] There are a few exceptions. Head Start has performance standards established by the Department of Health and Human Services, and programs receiving CCDBG funds are required to meet applicable state and local standards.

State child care standards for quality as well as health and safety are highly variable. This situation is partly due to the rapid growth of the market for child care and preschool programs resulting from the necessity of meeting the custodial care needs of working parents rather than in response to a clear educational or developmental philosophy for children. State licensing requirements for training of child care personnel, which has been strongly linked to improved outcomes for children, provide a case in point. California requires twelve credits of early childhood or child development courses for those in charge of groups of children. Alabama requires only that an individual be sixteen years old and able to read and write. Half the states do not require any preservice training or education for those in charge of early childhood classrooms, and only a quarter require more than ten hours of in-service training a year.[44] In addition, in most states, different agencies establish requirements for child care and early education teachers, depending on the auspices of the program. For example, while state departments of education set standards for certification of preschool teachers in public schools, state social service agencies or health departments establish personnel standards for child care centers.[45]

Health and safety is another area in which there is much variation from state to state. Despite the fact that every state regulates child care to some extent, 43 percent of all children in out-of-home care are unprotected by state safety standards. This is primarily because nearly half the states exempt family care homes serving five or fewer children, and thirty-six states exempt homes serving three or fewer children. This accounts for nearly three-fourths of all children in family care. Infants and toddlers are particularly affected by this situation because they tend to be cared for in smaller family care homes. Thirteen states currently exempt child care programs run by religious institutions from minimal standards of safety and quality, although such organizations operate about one-third of all child care centers.[46]

States also have very different regulations concerning quality standards in such areas as group size and adult-child ratio. Although child development experts recommend no more than three or four infants per caregiver, nineteen states allow child care centers to operate with five or more infants per adult, and thirteen states allow a single family child care provider to care for five or more infants and toddlers. In Idaho, a single caregiver can care for as many as twelve infants in a child care center. Nearly half of the states specify no maximum group size.[47]

In developing standards at the state or local level, it is important to recognize that different communities have very different cultures, resources, and needs with respect to child care. Distinctions should be made between the kinds of performance standards that provide goals for child care programs and intrusive regulations that impose overly costly requirements for physical space, for example. In a study of state regulations and their impact on child care availability, William Gormley found that regulations differ in their costliness, intrusiveness, and enforceability and that these characteristics have differing effects on the availability of care. He found that improving staff-child ratios may be too costly for center-based providers, whereas limitations on group size and requirements for staff training are more manageable. Gormley also suggests that states can help family care providers by streamlining their regulatory processes, elimi-

nating unnecessary regulations, and reducing routine inspections.[48]

States can also encourage quality improvements in family child care by expanding the role of resource and referral (R&R) agencies, rather than by imposing punitive regulatory requirements. These agencies could serve as networks for family care providers to promote the aspects of care quality that cannot be regulated, such as child-staff interaction and developmentally appropriate curriculums.[49]

We believe that there is a large public stake in providing protection for the health and safety of young children in out-of-home care because children cannot protect themselves and parents cannot continually monitor what is happening to their children while away from home. However, we believe that the states and localities are in the best position to adopt reasonable health, safety, and quality standards that do not place an undue burden on providers at the local level. We would encourage states to develop performance standards that reflect current professional knowledge of the characteristics that promote positive outcomes for young children in out-of-home care but to allow trade-offs among these standards. We also believe that federal funding for programs for low-income children should be contingent on local programs complying with state standards.

THE NEED FOR BETTER INFORMATION ON QUALITY

An important rationale for greater government intervention in child care is that a shortage of information is preventing the market from operating efficiently. Some observers have noted that it is very difficult for parents to determine the quality of care their children receive. The child care market is very decentralized, and most of the information about quality is obtained by word of mouth, which may or may not be reliable. A recent qualitative survey of parental attitudes toward child care revealed that many found looking for care so stressful that they usually settled on the first place that seemed acceptable, which often meant they had to find an alternative arrangement a short time thereafter.[50] This may be because it is generally both difficult and expensive for parents to get time off from work in order to visit a sufficient number of child care facilities. In one study of three cities, only half the parents using out-of-home care visited more than one provider before making a choice.[51] Once parents choose a child care setting, they must often rely on reports from their children, who are rarely able to communicate the level of quality accurately. Even if parents could spend more time observing a number of programs, many would still not choose higher quality because they often cannot know how the child care situation may affect their children later in life.

We believe that increased research and public education on the characteristics and costs of quality child care should be a top priority. Parents need better information on how to choose the most beneficial programs for their children, and they need assistance in locating care that is of decent quality, convenient, and affordable. This information should be coordinated with other information parents need in order to make informed choices and gain access to various forms of assistance.

Dayton Hudson, the Minneapolis-based retailer, has developed an extensive program to address the serious gap in information about child care. As an outgrowth of its long-established support of child care and other family-friendly corporate policies, Dayton

---

DAYTON HUDSON CORPORATION'S CHILD CARE QUALITY AWARENESS CAMPAIGN

The Dayton Hudson Corporation launched a $2.8 million public service advertising campaign called "Child Care Aware" to educate parents about the importance of child care quality. The company is promoting quality care by providing inserts with tips on quality in its Target and Mervyn's advertising sections in newspapers and through billboards and broadcast ads that offer parents a toll-free national hotline to call for referrals to local nonprofit child care resources. It is also publicizing the importance of quality care through in-store promotions at Mervyn's and Target stores. The in-store promotions include hang tags on products, a brochure on child care that can be picked up at the service desk and front checkout lanes, and lapel buttons worn by checkout clerks that say "I Care About Child Care" and that feature a picture of a baby. In-store events feature representatives from nonprofit child care resource and referral agencies. The campaign is sponsored by Dayton Hudson, its foundation, and its Target and Mervyn's stores and is being conducted with Bonneville Com-

munications of Salt Lake City, the Child Care Action Campaign, and several other child care advocacy and professional groups.

The campaign was developed as an outgrowth of the company's caregiver training program called "Family-to-Family." When 5,000 child care workers in sixteen states had been trained, they began reporting that demand for their services had not increased as a result of improved skills. Parents, they asserted, were most concerned with low cost and convenience rather than quality and were "so overwhelmed trying to juggle work and child-rearing duties that they make hasty and ill-considered choices." They did not care whether the caregiver was licensed or trained, although they associated top-notch caregivers with abilities that are associated with training and licensing. Because most parents adamantly oppose price increases, many child care centers are forced to cut teacher pay and increase class size, thereby lowering the quality of care.

SOURCE: Dayton Hudson Child Care Aware Campaign and *Wall Street Journal,* July 6, 1992

Hudson has initiated a major public information campaign called "Child Care Aware" throughout its Mervyn's and Target stores nationwide to educate parents about the importance of child care quality. Child Care Aware offers parents a useful checklist for judging the quality of the care they are using for their children.

The most important mechanism at the local level for bringing needed information to parents and coordinating resources for families and providers is R&R agencies. However, many R&Rs provide only minimal information about programs in their community, without attempting to rate the quality of the programs or assist parents in their choices.[52] In general, both federal and state funding for R&Rs is extremely limited, although about $41 million of the 1992 CCDBG allocation of $825 million is available to states for quality improvements that may, among other things, include R&R services. Some very successful R&R agencies are run in California, Massachusetts, and Michigan. The California initiative is a public-private partnership funded by the federal and state governments and corporations[53] (see Chapter 5, page 56).

We believe that expansion of resource and referral services is one of the most important ways to provide parents with information and assistance in locating quality child care. R&Rs can also act as networks for child care providers, particularly family care operators, to coordinate training opportunities, provide professional resources, and help isolated family care operators maintain regular contact with other providers. It is important, however, that R&Rs also provide substantive information about program quality and have the authority to make this information available to parents.

CHILD CARE QUALITY CHECKLIST

Basics:
- Is the program licensed or registered?
- Is the group's size OK for my child's age?
- Is the caregiver trained and experienced?

The Place:
- Is there enough space?
- Are there different places for different activities?
- Is the outdoor play area fenced, hazard-free, and completely visible to the caregiver?
- Is the space bright and pleasant?
- Is there an acceptable child-to-staff ratio?

Parents' Role:
- Are unannounced visits OK?
- Are there ways for you to get involved?

Do the Caregivers:
- Genuinely like children?
- Talk to children at their eye level?
- Share your beliefs about discipline?
- Greet your child when you arrive?
- Comfort children when needed?
- Keep you up to date on your child's activities?
- Make themselves available to answer your questions?

Activities:
- Are active and quiet experiences balanced?
- Are toys safe for each age, clean, and available?

SOURCE: Dayton Hudson Child Care Aware and *Wall Street Journal*, July 6, 1992

Chapter 5

BUILDING PUBLIC-PRIVATE PARTNERSHIPS FOR CHILD CARE DELIVERY

To most observers, the nation's system for delivering child care services is chaotic. It is a system that has grown haphazardly to meet burgeoning demand and, as a consequence, has little coherence for parents, providers, employers, and policy makers. Although the actual number of child care places seems to match the number of children needing care, there are many gaps in delivery that should be addressed through the development of a more coordinated and comprehensive system.

To a significant extent, large employers have taken the lead in attempting to improve the access of their employees to affordable, quality child care. Most early efforts were focused on meeting the needs of their own employees, but a growing trend among employers is to work singly or in collaboration with other companies and public- and private-sector agencies to improve child care delivery in the communities in which they operate. In this chapter, we examine the growing role business is playing in improving child care. We also look at some of the alternative models for improving delivery that are bringing the public and private sectors together to address child care needs.*

THE ROLE OF BUSINESS IN IMPROVING CHILD CARE

Companies all across the United States have come to recognize the benefits they can derive by helping employees meet their child care needs and other family obligations. In the past ten years, corporate involvement in child care has increased from an estimated 600 employers to about 5,600. Yet, this number still represents only 13 percent of the 44,000 U.S. employers with more than 100 employees.[1] The 1990 *National Child Care Survey* (NCCS) found that about half of all families receive some assistance from their employers to help them balance work and family needs.[2] This assistance takes many forms:

- R&R services to assist employees in locating child care in the community. This service is offered by 55 percent of large companies.

- Participation in the federal Dependent Care Assistance Plan (DCAP), which allows employees to use up to $5,000 of pretax income to purchase child care services. This tax plan is available in 50 percent of large companies.

- On-site or near-site child care centers. According to the NCCS, 10 percent of parents have access to child care through their or their spouse's place of employment;[3] the Families and Work Institute's estimate is that 13 percent of large companies maintain on- or near-site centers.

- Help with the cost of child care by arranging for discounts for their employees at local centers or providing vouchers to subsidize part of the cost.

- After-school care or summer programs for older children.

*See memorandum by LUCIO A. NOTO (page 68).

- Creating special arrangements with hospitals or emergency services to address the care needs of sick children.

- Offering generous parental leave so that parents can stay home during all or part of their child's first year. This benefit is offered to women by 28 percent of large companies and to men by 22 percent.

- Offering employees flextime, job sharing, or part-time positions to ease the transition back to work after leave time has ended.

In addition to these options for assisting employees in meeting their child care needs, companies are becoming involved in both limited and extensive public-private partnerships to upgrade the child care infrastructure in the communities in which they operate and their employees live. A variety of public-private partnerships are discussed later in this chapter, beginning on page 55.

Whatever approaches companies decide to take, each organization should first assess its own individual needs regarding child care in order to determine the best course of action.

The following sections describe examples of some creative responses companies are taking to help employees to balance work and family obligations more successfully.

ON-SITE AND NEAR-SITE CENTERS

About 900 of the nation's 1,400 on- or near-site child care centers are associated with hospitals; the rest are evenly split between corporations and government agencies. Although many think of on-site centers as an ideal child care solution, this option is either infeasible or inappropriate for most companies.[4]

Most companies with on-site or near-site child care subsidize the centers substantially. Parents usually are charged fees on a sliding scale based on income and age of child. The Campbell Soup Company, headquartered in Camden, New Jersey, underwrites approximately 40 percent of its center's operating budget. The center's capacity is 135 children.

Parents pay between $68 per week for kindergarten-age children and $88 per week for infants.[5] Champion International, a major paper company, also subsidizes child care for its employees at its headquarters site in Stamford, Connecticut (see "Corporate-Sponsored Child Care at Champion International," page 50).

A few companies, such as SAS Institute, Inc., a developer of computer software products, provide full subsidies. The two centers that SAS Institute operates at its headquarters in Cary, North Carolina, have a capacity of 328 children, and parents pay only the cost of their children's lunches and snacks, approximately $2 per day.[6]

An easier option for some companies is to contribute to a near-site child care center that serves the broader community. A Dow Chemical USA manufacturing plant in Plaquemine, Louisiana, contributes funding to a child care center run by River West Medical Center, a local hospital. In exchange for a first-year contribution of $25,000, Dow agreed to fill twenty-five slots and provide other in-kind support, such as periodic inspection by Dow's safety and security personnel to ensure the safety of the staff and children. Dow also provides monetary support for caregiver training and for vans for a summer camp program. The center has a total of seventy-two children (capacity for eighty-two), and 65 percent are children of Dow employees. The company subsidizes the center, and the Dow employees who use the center receive a discount of about 20 percent over the rates paid by nonemployees.[7]

Stride Rite Corporation, a manufacturer of shoes for children and adults, has had on-site child care since 1971. In 1990, one of the two centers expanded to include elder care. The Stride Rite Intergenerational Center has the capacity for fifty-five children and twenty-four elders. The program aims to meet the physical, social, and intellectual needs of both children and elders through a carefully planned and supervised curriculum that fosters regular daily contact between the two groups. For

CORPORATE-SPONSORED CHILD CARE AT CHAMPION INTERNATIONAL

For Andrew C. Sigler, the chairman and chief executive officer of Champion International Corporation, having a company respond to the needs of its employees makes good business sense. Among the progressive employee benefits Champion offers are company fitness centers and generous family leave policies.

"Why do we do all these things?" asks Sigler. "To be more competitive." With this philosophy in mind, Champion initiated a child care program at its Stamford, Connecticut, location to improve productivity, attract top-notch employees, and improve the attitude of employees toward the company. With nearly 500 employees at the headquarters location, a child care program made sense.

Beginning in the early 1980s, the company looked at other programs in the area, and all failed to meet Champion's standards. It also tried to form partnerships with the Stamford school system and other businesses, but nothing came of these efforts. After two failed attempts, says Sigler, the company decided to put together its own child care program.

Champion designated a building across the street as the child care center, contracted with the King Low-Heywood Thomas Schools to manage it, and hired a director and an architect. Every aspect of the center was designed to meet the developmental needs of children. The center has a capacity for sixty children from ages three months to five years. It pays center employees on a scale comparable to the lower end of Stamford school district salaries and provides benefits, though not full Champion benefits. Start-up costs were approximately a half million dollars, and the annual operating budget is around $600,000. Champion charges parents $135 a week for the oldest child and $175 for infants. Called the Downtown Children's Center, Champion's program also accepts children whose parents are not employees, although it charges them considerably more.

The center has experienced no employee turnover problems or legal problems; only the high cost of quality care remains a difficulty. Champion subsidized the center with $175,000 in 1990 but considers it worth it. Because the company has a child care center, says Sigler, it has been able to attract top-rate local people. Other Champion locations are also addressing child care needs. In Hamilton, Ohio, for example, Champion has an arrangement with local hospitals so that if a child is sick, the parent can bring the child to the hospital infirmary and does not have to lose a day of work. The Hamilton facility is also trying to set up an after-school program for older children.

Mr. Sigler feels that the only way a company can start a child care program like Champion's is to have support from the top level of the corporation. He is very pleased with the Champion child care program — not only from a corporate perspective but also for the sake of the children the program benefits.

SOURCE: Champion International

child care, parents who are Stride Rite employees are charged on a sliding fee scale based on household income; employees are given a discount on the cost of elder care. Half of the child and elder care slots are available to the community. Low-income families receive a subsidy for child or elder care.

Providing on- or near-site child care is not limited to large companies. Bowles Corporation, an engineering firm with only twelve employees, started providing child care in the office in 1986, when two of its employees were unable to find suitable arrangements. The center has grown and has been relocated to a mobile home on company grounds. It employs two child care workers and serves twelve children; seven are children of employees, and five are children of community residents.[8]

Employer Liability. One barrier to establishing child care centers often cited by companies is the problem of liability. In a 1989 report to the U.S. Department of Labor, the Child Care Liability Insurance Task Force concluded that employers who maintain on-site and near-site child care centers do not perceive liability as much of a problem and believe that risk reduction is relatively easy to accomplish, whereas employers without child care centers worry most about liability and the cost of insurance. Although these responses may reflect some genuine differences in circumstances, there is some evidence that the difficulties imposed by liability are overestimated. In one study, employers who had not looked into insurance costs were found to estimate them to be six times higher than actual levels. The task force found that in reality, the average cost of insurance for an employer-sponsored center is 1 to 3 percent of a center's operating budget, or less than one week's tuition in most cases. Nevertheless, the task force cautioned that other segments of the child care market, particularly family care homes, may not enjoy the same access to affordable liability insurance.[9]

FAMILY CARE INITIATIVES

A more practical option for most companies is to try to enhance the supply of family child care homes. American Express and the Dayton Hudson subsidiaries Mervyn's and Target have significant initiatives in this area. American Express funds family child care associations and R&R agencies to recruit and train new providers and help them get licensed.[10]

The Home-Based Care program that is run by America West Airlines in eight locations around the country provides a network of family child care homes for its employees. Providers, who are independent contractors, may care for no more than four unrelated children and no more than two children under the age of two. America West manages the program, supervising recruitment, training, and monthly inspections. The company also sponsors a toy-lending library, and monthly visits by a trained specialist provide support to the caregiver, offer new creative activities for the children, and ensure compliance with program standards. Caregivers must pass courses in pediatric first aid and cardiopulmonary resuscitation (CPR). America West provides a subsidy to parents of between 25 and 50 percent, and weekly fees average between $75 and $80 for full-time care.[11]

EMERGENCY CHILD CARE SERVICES

One of the most difficult forms of help for parents to locate is emergency care for a sick child. Company sick leave policies rarely allow parents to take time off to care for a sick child, and parents often have to lie in order to do so. Even when parents have good child care arrangements, children who are too sick to attend their regular family care home or center must be attended to at home. In recognition of this problem, a group of fifteen companies in New York City formed the Emergency Child Care Services (ECCS) initiative. Spearheaded by Time Warner Inc., the program offers at-home care for up to three consecutive days to children under the age of thirteen who cannot attend school or their regular child care because of illness or other emergencies. Its purpose is to address short-term child care needs for employees who cannot be absent from work.[12]

AFTER-SCHOOL AND HOLIDAY CARE

A number of companies are now helping parents meet the special care needs of school-age children during vacation and holiday periods. John Hancock Mutual Life Insurance Company's Kids-to-Go program offers field trips and other activities around the Boston area for children from six to thirteen. Parents pay $25 per day, which covers admission charges to museums and other locations, as well as transportation. "Scholarships" are available to cover up to 50 percent of the cost for John Hancock employees who earn less than $30,000 per year.[13]

Bausch & Lomb, a manufacturer of precision opticals in Rochester, New York, runs a camp called Kids Club for school-age children of employees during school holidays and summers. The company subsidizes the $90-a-week fee based on household income.

CREATING FAMILY-FRIENDLY WORKPLACES

Studies by the Families and Work Institute have demonstrated that companies go through a number of evolutionary stages in the development of workplaces that are more friendly toward employees who must juggle work and family obligations. Companies often start out with single-strategy responses, such as offering child care R&R services, a DCAP, or even an on-site center. But with experience and changes in philosophy, companies often expand their vision of what it means to maintain a family-friendly work environment and develop a more comprehensive and coordinated policy agenda.

The institute notes that companies generally go through three distinct stages: In stage 1, companies develop a pragmatic approach to providing a specific benefit, usually some form of child care assistance to meet a need they have determined to be of particular importance to employees. In stage 2, companies will develop an integrated approach to work-family benefits. In stage 3, they recognize that innovative work-family policies can flourish only in a supportive corporate culture. Among companies that are known for having highly supportive family-friendly workplaces are Corning Incorporated, IBM (see page 53), and Johnson & Johnson (see page 54).

NEW APPROACHES TO CHILD CARE DELIVERY

Several alternative approaches have been developed by experts in the field of early childhood education and care to improve the delivery of services at the local level. Each model is built on a different organizing principle. The Resource Center model takes a community-centered approach that relies on R&R agencies to provide coordination, training, and referral. The "School of the 21st Century" would place the major institutional burden for organizing and coordinating child care services on schools. A third model is based on the concept of public-

CORNING INCORPORATED

Corning Incorporated, a maker of glass and ceramic products that also runs clinical testing labs, developed a framework of family-friendly policies when James R. Houghton took over as chief executive officer in 1983. In an effort to improve its financial position, Mr. Houghton focused the company on improving quality and identified its employees as the key to this effort. Corning's managers were charged with helping their employees balance their work and family responsibilities.

Corning has built on this family-friendly base with programs to promote diversity. It established permanent Quality Improvement Teams (QITs) to identify barriers to advancement for women and minorities and recommend ways to eliminate them. The company also created a mentor program to identify women and minorities with potential and help them chart their career paths.

Its family-friendly work environment has helped Corning cut the turnover rate among women managers in half. Corning currently provides two child care centers near its corporate headquarters in Rochester and supports near-site centers in other locations. It also supports YMCA summer camps, before-and after-school programs, and emergency child care and participates in the DCAP to help employees reduce their child care expenses. Corning also provides up to six months of leave for childbirth, for both new mothers and fathers, and leave for family illness. Adoptive parents also have leave available and up to $2,000 per child in adoption aid. The company provides free access to an R&R service. The family care specialist on the hotline gives information on Corning's family-friendly programs and advice on child care, adoption, and parenting. Corning also offers a variety of alternative work schedules, such as job sharing, work at home, and compressed workweeks, to help parents balance work with family life.

SOURCE: Corning Incorporated and *The Corporate Reference Guide to Work-Family Programs*

private partnership. One example of such a partnership is a Child Care Investment Fund that would combine public and private resources and distribute them on a matching basis to locally initiated child care projects.

What each of these approaches has in common is a central philosophy of public-private partnership which recognizes that government, business, and parents have a vested interest in creating a delivery system for child care and early education that meets the diverse needs of communities.

RESOURCE CENTER MODEL

Developed by Gwen Morgan, a professor of early childhood education at Wheelock College, this delivery system for child care is organized around a community-based Resource Center that supports parents, providers, and the community.[14] This approach recognizes that good-quality child care already exists in many communities but that this base needs to be built upon to ensure that overall quality is strength-

ened, that additional funding sources are found, that child care services match demand, and that parents are assured of finding accessible and affordable quality care for their children.

This community-based system would exert a minimum of bureaucratic control and would not centralize the management of programs. Resource Centers would be nonprofit organizations and would receive both public and private funds.

Elements of the Resource Center model are being implemented in Massachusetts and California. It is also currently being implemented in Maryland, with the strong support of the Maryland Employers Advisory Council on Child Care. Designated "The Maryland Child Care Resource Center Network," its primary goal is to improve the availability and the affordability of quality child care programs throughout the state by creating a private, nonprofit network of community-based Child Care Resource Centers (CCRCs) that perform the following functions:

IBM

IBM was one of the first companies to recognize the implications of the changing demographics of the work force and to help its employees deal with the issue of balancing work and family. The company's approach is based on its three guiding principles: respect for the individual, good corporate citizenship, and the pursuit of excellence.

In 1984, IBM created the first nationwide child care R&R service, which was emulated by other companies. The goal was not only to provide information on where to find child care but also to help create new child care programs to meet the needs of employees and to monitor the quality of the care. In November 1989, IBM established a $22 million fund to help increase the supply and quality of child care services where IBM employees live or work.

IBM also has several programs to help par-

ents cope with other family-related issues. The company provides financial assistance of up to $50,000 per child to the parents of emotionally, physically, and mentally disabled children. It also offers adoption assistance information and reimburses employees for up to 80 percent of adoption costs or $2,500. Moreover, the company has established a SchoolSmart program to help parents become more effective in helping their children succeed in school. Other benefits include work and family seminars to help parents balance their work and family responsibilities, flexibility in arranging work schedules, and a video library for office or home use with videos on topics such as AIDS and teenage substance abuse. The company was one of the first to institute a management training program to sensitize managers to work and family problems and familiarize them with IBM's policies.

SOURCE: IBM and *The Corporate Reference Guide to Work-Family Programs*

- Identify child care needs and develop more child care resources
- Advise parents regarding available child care options
- Provide technical assistance to established and prospective child care providers and employers

JOHNSON & JOHNSON

Johnson & Johnson launched its "Balancing Work & Family" initiative in early 1989. The company had offered some family-friendly programs since the early 1980s through its LIVE FOR LIFE program; but in 1987, it noticed the demographics of its work force had shifted from almost exclusively male to a growing proportion of women with children under six and minorities. The company realized it needed to implement a more comprehensive work and family agenda to remain competitive, to attract and retain top-quality employees, and to maintain its image as a family-friendly company.

Among the programs included in the Johnson & Johnson Balancing Work & Family initiative are:

- A program to train supervisors to handle work and family issues
- Three on-site child development centers, with others in the planning stage, and support of other near-site centers
- Programs to help families find the best schools for their children and a School-Smart program that offers advice to parents on helping their child achieve in school
- Participation in the DCAP, which allows employees to use pretax dollars to meet expenses relating to child or elder care
- Unpaid family leave of up to one year with a guaranteed job on return
- A child and elder care referral service
- Adoption assistance covering up to $3,000 in expenses

SOURCE: Johnson & Johnson and *The Corporate Reference Guide to Work-Family Programs*

- Increase pubic awareness about child care issues

The council envisions a network of Resource Centers in the ten regions of the state and a private, nonprofit Statewide Child Care Resource Center (SCCRC) to provide coordination and technical assistance to the CCRCs. Each CCRC and the SCCRC would have community-based advisory boards, and funding would come from a combination of public and private sources, including fees for services. CCRC services would include the recruitment of new providers, child care R&R counseling, technical assistance for employers as well as for current and prospective child care providers, training for providers, and parent education. The council has initiated a three-year demonstration project to start up and refine the Maryland network, with three centers initially established in an urban, a suburban, and a rural setting.

PUBLIC SCHOOLS AS A HUB FOR CHILD CARE

Another approach, which is being tried in a number of communities, proposes to use the public schools as the hub of a comprehensive child care system, replacing the current patchwork of programs. The best-known example of this approach is the School of the 21st Century, proposed by Edward Zigler, a founder of Head Start.[15] The School of the 21st Century is being implemented in school districts in Missouri, Connecticut, Wyoming, Colorado, Texas, Iowa, and other states around the nation, and a design team headed by Dr. Zigler has recently been awarded a grant by the New American Schools Development Corporation to expand the model to additional school districts.

The School of the 21st Century would provide child care for three- to five-year-olds at the school site along with before- and after-school care and vacation care for children between five and twelve. Teachers would be specially certified in early childhood education; and the curriculum would be developmentally appropriate, not academically based. Parents would be charged fees on a sliding scale.

Children under age three would be cared for in family child care homes, by relatives, or by parents themselves. R&R services would help parents with special needs find appropriate care.

Connecting child care to elementary schools makes a great deal of sense. Schools are established institutions within the community and therefore accessible to parents. Greater integration of children from a variety of economic classes and racial and cultural groups is possible. A developmentally based curriculum for preschoolers can also be used to reorganize curriculums in the early elementary grades, which many early childhood experts believe are too academically oriented now.

There are also a number of drawbacks that make this approach impractical as a national model. First, the cost may be prohibitively high. Dr. Zigler estimates that the total cost of such a system on a national basis would be $75 to $100 billion, four to five times more than consumers and the government together currently spend on child care.[16] Second, the school-based model fails to incorporate existing community-based public and private nonprofit and for-profit child care centers, which largely serve preschool children now and provide an infrastructure that should be built upon. Third, the availability of school facilities can be limited or variable, making it difficult to house the program. Many schools in older urban areas are in terrible condition and unsafe for the students currently attending them, much less preschoolers.

PUBLIC-PRIVATE PARTNERSHIPS

In most communities, business is more likely to become involved in providing child care or upgrading existing care opportunities if there already is government support and an existing child care infrastructure.[17] A good deal of government effort has gone into trying to stimulate greater business involvement in child care. Bills offering tax credits to employers have been passed in thirteen states, but very few of these efforts have resulted in corporate interest in on-site programs. According to Ellen Galinsky and Dana Friedman of the Families and Work Institute, the reason for this low response is that most businesses prefer to help their employees pay for existing community-based care services rather than create their own.[18]

Although companies are concerned primarily with meeting the child care needs of their own employees, they have increasingly concluded that they can best accomplish this goal by engaging in a variety of public-private partnerships designed to help to improve both the supply and the quality of child care in their operating communities.

Such partnerships come in many forms. They may be limited to solving a specific child care problem for their employees or the community, or they may be more extensive and systemic in scope. Partnership may involve single companies or consortiums of companies working exclusively with child care providers, or they may involve a broad array of public agencies and community leaders.

Examples of extensive partnership initiatives undertaken by single companies include the AT&T Family Care Development Fund and the Dayton Hudson initiative to improve family child care. The purpose of the AT&T fund, established in 1989, is to increase the supply and improve the quality of child and elder care resources in communities throughout the country where AT&T employees live and work. The fund is part of a comprehensive work and families benefits package negotiated by AT&T, the Communications Workers of America (CWA), and the International Brotherhood of Electrical Workers (IBEW). The fund will invest up to $25 million over a six-year period (1990 to 1995). All projects receiving grants must directly benefit both AT&T employees and the community, and an employee must be involved with the project. In its first three years, the fund invested $10 million in more than 380 projects in twenty-six states. Moreover, the fund has enabled 200 child care providers to begin the process of earning accreditation from the National Association for the Educaton of Young Children (NAEYC).[19]

In thirty-two communities, Dayton Hudson and its retail store chains Mervyn's and Target have established "Family-to-Family" programs to recruit, train, and provide credentials for family child care providers and to conduct consumer education campaigns on the importance of selecting quality care.

In Colorado, Children's World Learning Centers, a major child care provider that is a subsidiary of ARA Services, has joined in partnership with a coalition of educational organizations and government agencies. Children's World provides space in one of its centers to Head Start, the State Department of Social Services, Employment Training Services, and Red Rocks Community College. Head Start uses one of the center's five classrooms for its preschool program. A second classroom is used as an adult training center for literacy programs, job skills, and basic parenting classes. In addition, Children's World provides care for children whose parents are attending classes at the center as well as full-day care for other children who receive subsidies from Social Services.

Examples of consortium ventures include efforts in Charlotte (North Carolina), Dallas-Fort Worth (Texas), Rochester (New York), and Minneapolis (Minnesota). In Charlotte, a joint venture among IBM, American Express, Allstate, Duke Power, and University Research Park built a $2 million child care center that exceeds state standards and is open to members of the community as well as employees of the companies. In Dallas-Forth Worth, IBM and Travelers Corporation established a $375,000 program to recruit and train family child care providers. The program has recruited seventy-five new home care providers, each of whom can care for four to six children. In Rochester, Eastman Kodak, Xerox, Bausch & Lomb, Blue Cross/Blue Shield, and others are offering training and low-cost group health insurance for child care workers. And in Minneapolis, Honeywell, First Bank System, 3M, and twelve other companies have created a system of referral services and subsidized in-home care for sick children.[20]

In September 1992, a historic, large-scale collaboration of major corporations, called the American Business Collaboration for Quality Dependent Care, was announced to address the child care needs of both employees and community residents across the country.

A number of extensive public-private partnerships have been operating in states and at the local level for some time. The California Child Care Initiative Project (CCCIP) was

---

AMERICAN BUSINESS COLLABORATION FOR QUALITY DEPENDENT CARE

A consortium of 137 major U.S. companies, initiated by IBM and including 11 of the nation's leading companies, has been created to provide a coast-to-coast network of child and elder care services for their employees and, in some cases, nonemployees. The consortium, called the American Business Collaboration for Quality Dependent Care (ABC), has raised $25.4 million to increase the supply and improve the quality of dependent care in 300 local programs in forty-four communities in twenty-five states and the District of Columbia. Programs targeted for the funds include new and expanded child care centers, programs for school-age children, in-home care for the elderly, and training for family child care providers.

The 10 blue-chip companies that are actively involved in the consortium with IBM are American Telephone & Telegraph, American Express, Xerox Corporation, Exxon Corporation, Eastman Kodak Company, Travelers Corporation, Johnson & Johnson, Amoco Corporation, the Allstate unit of Sears, Roebuck, and Motorola Inc. The consortium expects the initial costs will be offset by increased employee productivity.

SOURCE: IBM and Families and Work Institute

developed by the BankAmerica Foundation to address the shortage of licensed quality care in the state. The partnership involves thirty-three organizations (ten public agencies and twenty-three private funders) and relies on existing nonprofit R&R agencies to recruit and train family care providers. Between the program's inception in 1985 and 1991, funders have contributed $3.2 million. The project is now administered by the San Francisco Foundation. The California Child Care Resource and Referral Network, a statewide support group for R&Rs, manages its day-to-day activities. In its evaluation study of the success of the initiative, one California county found that providers who were trained through the CCCIP were more likely to join the local family child care association, participate in the Child Care Food Program, use book-lending services and borrow toys and equipment offered by the R&Rs, and seek additional training.[21]

The Oregon Child Care Initiative was established in 1988 by a group of child care professionals, parents, educators, and employers in an attempt to replicate the California initiative. Funding was provided by Mervyn's, a department store chain and subsidiary of Dayton Hudson, and the Ford Foundation. The Oregon Community Foundation also contributed funds to help market the program. By June 1990, the Oregon initiative had raised over $440,000, which has enabled it to train 400 providers and recruit another 151 new providers.[22] Another type of public-private partnership is the Child Care Investment Fund developed for the state of New York.

Although each public-private partnership is unique, there are certain elements they all need to hold in common to be successful. The Families and Work Institute has developed a set of guidelines that all public and private partners should follow when considering involvement in a child care partnership (see "Guidelines for Public-Private Partnerships for Child Care," page 58).

CHILD CARE INVESTMENT FUND

The Child Care Investment Fund is the centerpiece of an initiative developed by the Families and Work Institute to foster an ongoing public-private partnership for improving child care quality and delivery in New York State. The fund would be available to both nonprofit and profit-making programs, local government agencies, other community entities, and networks or associations of family child care providers.

Grant recipients would have to match $2 to every $1 from the fund, although resources would be targeted to low-income communities by reducing the fund match to $1 local for every $1 from the fund. The purpose of the grants would be to increase the supply and quality of child care at the local level. The fund itself is designed to support local initiative and flexibility, in recognition of the diversity of child care needs and preferences.

It is envisioned that the local matching money would be contributed by a variety of private-sector sources, including businesses, the United Way, chambers of commerce, local foundations, and colleges and universities.

SOURCE: Families and Work Institute

GUIDELINES FOR PUBLIC-PRIVATE PARTNERSHIPS FOR CHILD CARE

The Families and Work Institute offers a number of principles to guide development of a public-private partnership for child care.

- Identify champions who are strong, visible leaders with the ability to generate broad support from others in the community.
- Maintain flexibility to ensure that partnerships are responsive to the particular needs of diverse communities.
- Foster creativity among partners who can contribute money or services according to their abilities.
- Define clear goals and expectations at the outset of the partnership.
- Market the initiative in a specific, business-like manner, demonstrating that participation in a child care partnership represents an important investment.

- Pay attention to process as well as outcomes, so that the relationships among the various partners can lead to a stronger and longer-term commitment.
- Maintain a local focus, which gives the partners an immediate stake in results and ownership of the project.
- Develop ongoing communications to share news and reach potential new partners.
- Offer training and technical assistance to partners to help them learn to work together to achieve their mutual goals.
- Build in an evaluation component, which can help others replicate the partnership as well as strengthen the existing project.

SOURCE: Families and Work Institute

APPENDIX

MAJOR FEDERAL CHILD CARE PROGRAMS

DEPENDENT CARE TAX CREDIT

The DCTC is a nonrefundable credit against income tax liability for up to 30 percent of a limited amount of employment-related dependent care expenses. Qualified dependents include children under the age of thirteen, a physically or mentally incapacitated dependent of any age, and an incapacitated spouse. The cost of care must be incurred to allow the taxpayer or spouse to work, and it cannot exceed earned income or the income of the lesser-paid spouse. The maximum eligible dependent care expense is $2,400 for one qualified dependent and $4,800 for two or more.

The amount of the credit depends on adjusted gross income (AGI); and the ceiling is 30 percent for income under $10,000, with a maximum cash value of $720 for one dependent and $1,440 for two or more. The value of the credit is reduced by 1 percent for each additional $2,000 of AGI over $10,000, until at $28,000 the credit equals 20 percent for all incomes above this level.

In order to claim the credit, the taxpayer must report the correct name, address, and social security number or taxpayer identification number of the provider. The amount of expenses eligible for the dependent care tax credit is reduced, dollar for dollar, by the amount of expenses excluded from the taxpayer's income under the Dependent Care Asistance Program, which allows up to $5,000 to be deducted from gross income. In general, the tax credit is less valuable than the exclusion for taxpayers above the 15 percent tax bracket.

CHILD CARE AND DEVELOPMENT BLOCK GRANT

This program was legislated in 1990 and gives funds to states to provide child care services and improve the quality of those services. The funds are distributed to states based on the proportion of children under age five, the number of children receiving free or reduced-price lunches, and the state's per capita income. States do not have to match funds. The program was authorized through 1995 at the following levels: 1991, $750 million; 1992, $825 million; 1993, $925 million; and 1994-1995, to be determined.

States have considerable flexibility in how they can use the funds, but certain federal guidelines must be followed.

1. Seventy-five percent of the funds must be used to provide child care services to eligible children on a sliding fee scale according to income. Eligible children are those younger than thirteen whose family income does not exceed 75 percent of the state's median income and whose parents are working or attending a job training or educational program. Priority is given to families with the lowest incomes or special needs.

2. Of the remaining 25 percent, about 19 percent of the funds are to be used to increase the availability of early childhood development programs and before- and after-school care. Five percent is for quality improvements, which may include one or more of the following: an R&R program, grants or loans to providers to meet state and local standards, improvements in enforcement of or compliance with standards, training,

and salary improvement for staff. The remaining 1 percent of the funds may be put to any of these uses.

3. States must give all eligible families the option of either enrolling children with an eligible provider that has a grant from or contract with the block grant program or receiving a child care certificate that they can use to purchase child care.

4. All providers who receive the funding must be registered with the state, comply with all applicable state and local laws, and meet minimum health and safety standards.

SOCIAL SERVICES BLOCK GRANT, TITLE XX (SSBG)

Authorized in 1977 under Title XX of the Social Security Act, the SSBG allocates federal funds directly to states for a broad variety of social services. The amount received is based on population, with no state matching funds required. Most states use a portion of these funds to provide child care services. Although in general there are few restrictions on how the money can be applied, the federal government guidelines prohibit using funds for child care programs that do not meet state and local standards. According to the American Public Welfare Association, the thirty states that report use of the grants spend approximately 15.3 percent on child care services. In 1992, $2.6 billion was allocated through the SSBG, which was a decline in real terms of $3.2 billion, or 55 percent, since 1977.

DEPENDENT CARE ASSISTANCE PROGRAM (DCAP)

Also known as the Dependent Care Exclusion, this tax program allows employees of participating companies to exclude up to $5,000 per year in child or other dependent care expenses from gross income. Employees must report the social security number of the child care provider. The DCAP is generally more valuable than the DCTC for families above the 15 percent tax bracket; above $18,000, the maxi-

mum tax credit would be 20 percent of the cost of care up to $2,400. Furthermore, the amount of child care expenses eligible for the DCTC is reduced dollar for dollar by the amount excluded from income under the DCAP. Although the DCAP potentially provides a much greater financial subsidy to higher-income families, the current utilization is small compared with the tax credit, and the total amount received by families through the DCAP program is $65 million, compared with $4 billion through the tax credit.

FAMILY SUPPORT ACT (FSA)

Established in 1988, the Family Support Act represented a major welfare reform effort that focuses on moving adults from the welfare rolls into the paid work force. The FSA recognizes that child care assistance is a necessary part of this strategy. The act contains two separate provisions to address different aspects of this need.

- **AFDC Child Care Program.** States are required to guarantee child care to AFDC recipients if it is needed for an individual to accept employment, to remain employed, or to participate in a state-approved education or training program.

- **Transitional Child Care Assistance.** States must provide child care assistance to families who leave AFDC because of increased earnings, hours of work, or loss of earning disregards in the calculation of AFDC eligibility. To be eligible for transitional assistance, families must have received AFDC in at least three of the previous six months. There is no federally mandated income limit; states determine the amount of a family's copayment based on a state-designed sliding-scale formula according to income.

AT-RISK CHILD CARE PROGRAM

This program gives states matching funds to help them provide child care services to low-income working parents who are not currently receiving AFDC but who would be at risk of becoming eligible for welfare if child care were not available. States set the income limit for the program, and families are expected to contribute to the cost of care based on a state-designated sliding fee scale. Unlike the AFDC and Transitional Child Care (TCC) programs, child care providers that are exempted from state and local regulations must register with the state to receive these funds.

CHILD CARE FOOD PROGRAM

The Child Care Food Program provides federal assistance for meals served to children in licensed care centers and family care homes. The majority of children served are between three and five, although older children are eligible. In fiscal 1992, the program was funded at $1.2 billion. It is administered by the U.S. Department of Agriculture.

To be eligible, at least 25 percent of the children in a center must receive support under the SSBG. Centers can be either nonprofit or for-profit. All children in qualifying centers can receive subsidized meals regardless of family income, but reimbursement rates vary with income on the same scale as the school lunch program. For family child care, there is no income test for meals, and all meals and snacks are subsidized at the same rate.

HEAD START

Head Start is a comprehensive child development program administered by the Administration for Children, Youth and Families in the Department of Health and Human Services. Its goals are to improve the social competence, learning skills, and health and nutrition status of low-income children ages three to five. Although Head Start is often thought of as a federal child care program for poor children, the vast majority (91 percent) of Head Start programs offer only part-day and part-year services. In addition, there are fairly rigorous parent-involvement requirements that make it difficult, if not impossible, for many

children with working parents to participate in the program.

At least 90 percent of the children served in a Head Start program must come from families with incomes at or below the state poverty line, and at least 10 percent of the enrollment slots must be reserved for disabled children. Grants are awarded by Department of Health and Human Services regional agencies to public agencies, nonprofit organizations, and local school systems.

During the 1990-1991 school year, approximately 50 percent of Head Start families were receiving AFDC benefits, and about 71 percent had incomes of less than $9,000 per year. Forty-five percent of the household heads in Head Start families were unemployed, and 33 percent were employed full time.

ADDITIONAL INCOME SUPPLEMENT PROGRAMS FOR FAMILIES

Earned Income Tax Credit (EITC). The Earned Income Tax Credit is not meant to offer direct assistance for child care; but like the DCTC, it provides work incentives and an income supplement for families with children under age nineteen. Unlike the DCTC, the EITC is refundable; so even if a family has no tax liability, it will receive a benefit from this program. Eligible low-income workers could claim a credit of up to 17.6 percent (18.4 percent for more than one child) of the first $7,570 of earned income for 1992. The maximum credit amount in 1992 was $1,324 for one child, and the credit was phased out for workers with earned income over $22,370.

Supplemental Newborn Tax Credit. An additional supplemental credit is available for children under one year of age at the end of the calendar year. In 1992, the supplemental credit was 5 percent of the first $7,520 of earned income, and the maximum credit is $376. A taxpayer may not also claim the DCTC for any child for whom the individual receives this supplemental credit.

NOTES

CHAPTER 1

1. Congressional Economic Leadership Institute, *A Briefing for the Congressional Competitiveness Caucus* (Washington, D.C., September 1992).

2. Barbara Willer, *The Demand and Supply of Child Care in 1990* (Washington, D.C.: National Association for the Education of Young Children, 1991).

3. Center for the Study of Social Policy, *The Challenge of Change: What the 1990 Census Tells Us About Children* (Washington, D.C., September 1992), Tables 21 and 22, pp. 42-43.

4. Frank Levy and Richard Michel, *The Economic Future of American Families* (Washington, D.C.: The Urban Institute Press, 1991), pp. 35-42.

5. When saving is defined as the increase in net worth.

6. Sandra L. Hanson and Theodora Ooms, "The Economic Costs and Rewards of Two-Earner, Two-Parent Families," *Journal of Marriage and Family* 53 (August 1991), and Bureau of Labor Statistics.

7. Hanson and Ooms, "The Economic Costs and Rewards of Two-Earner, Two-Parent Families."

8. *Embracing Our Future: A Child Care Action Agenda* (Boston: The Boston Foundation, Carol R. Goldberg Seminar on Child Care, 1992), p. 54.

9. Hanson and Ooms, "The Economic Costs and Rewards of Two-Earner, Two-Parent Families."

10. *Embracing Our Future.*

11. Victor R. Fuchs, *Women's Quest for Economic Equality* (Cambridge: Harvard University Press, 1988), p. 111.

12. Committee for Economic Development, *An America That Works: The Life-Cycle Approach to a Competitive Work Force* (1990), p. 20.

13. Ellen Galinsky and Dana Friedman, *Education Before School: Investing in Quality Child Care*, A Study Prepared for the Committee for Economic Development (New York: Scholastic Inc., 1993), p. 15.

14. Galinsky and Friedman, *Education Before School*, p. 58.

15. Sandra L. Hofferth et al., *National Child Care Survey, 1990*, A National Association for the Education of Young Children Study (Washington, D.C.: The Urban Institute Press, 1991), p. 346.

16. Galinsky and Friedman, *Education Before School*, p. 67.

17. Galinsky and Friedman, *Education Before School*, p. 125.

18. James S. Coleman, *Policy Perspectives: Parental Involvement in Education* (Washington, D.C.: U.S. Department of Education, Office of Education Research and Information, U.S. Government Printing Office, June 1991).

19. Hofferth et al., *National Child Care Survey, 1990*, p. 99.

20. Coleman, *Policy Perspectives.*

21. Urie Bronfenbrenner, "Strengthening Family Systems," in *The Parental Leave Crisis*, ed. Edward F. Zigler and Meryl Frank (New Haven: Yale University Press, 1988), pp. 143-160.

22. Unpublished tabulations from *March 1991 Current Population Survey* and *March 1976 Current Population Survey*, U.S. Department of Labor, Bureau of Labor Statistics.

23. Bureau of Labor Statistics.

24. Willer et al., *The Demand and Supply of Child Care in 1990*, p. 8.

25. Center for the Study of Social Policy, *The Challenge of Change*, p. 23.

26. Center for the Study of Social Policy, *The Challenge of Change*, pp. 46-47.

27. Center for the Study of Social Policy, *The Challenge of Change*, p. 20.

28. Committee for Economic Development, *The Unfinished Agenda: A New Vision for Child Development and Education* (1991), p. 9.

29. National Center for Children in Poverty, *Five Million Children: 1992 Update* (New York: Columbia University, School of Public Health, 1992).

30. CED estimates. The value of all unpaid household work in 1975 has been estimated at 33.7 percent of GNP in R. Eisner, *The Total Incomes System of Accounts*, Appendix A, pp. 55-76. Eisner's time budgets suggest that child care represented about 15 percent of this total, or 5 percent of GNP in 1975. However, both the value of unpaid household work relative to GNP and the proportion of such work devoted to child care have declined in the eighteen years since then.

31. R. Maynard and E. McGinnis, "Policies to Enhance Access to High-Quality Child Care," in *Child Care in the 1990s: Trends and Consequences*, ed. A. Booth (Hillsdale, N.J.: Lawrence Erlbaum Associates, 1992), p. 193

32. Deborah Lowe Vandell and Janaki Ramanan, "Effects of Early and Recent Maternal Employment on Children from Low-Income Families," *Child Development* 63 (1992): 938-949.

33. J. S. Fuerst and Dorothy Fuerst, "Chicago Experience with Early Childhood Program: The Special Case of the Child Parent Center Program," *Urban Education* 28, No. 1 (April 1993), and Dominic F. Gullo, *The Effects of Gender, At-Risk Status, and Number of Years in Preschool on Children's Academic Readiness* (Mil-

waukee: University of Wisconsin-Milwaukee, Department of Early Childhood Education, 1990).

34. Galinsky and Friedman, *Education Before School*, p. 47.

CHAPTER 2

1. The Report of the National Task Force on School Readiness, *Caring Communities: Supporting Young Children and Families* (Alexandria, Va.: National Association of State Boards of Education, December 1991).

2. Gary Natriello, Edward L. McDill, and Aaron M. Pallas, *Schooling Disadvantaged Children: Racing Against Catastrophe* (New York: Teachers College, Columbia University, 1990), pp. 30-32.

3. Ellen Kisker and Rebecca Maynard, "Quality, Cost, and Parental Choice of Child Care," in *The Economics of Child Care*, ed. David M. Blau (New York: Russell Sage Foundation, New York, 1991), pp. 128-130.

4. Kisker and Maynard, "Quality, Cost, and Parental Choice of Child Care," pp. 129-130.

5. Cheryl D. Hayes, John L. Palmer, and Martha J. Zaslow, eds., *Who Cares for America's Children?* (Washington, D.C.: Panel on Child Care Policy, National Research Council, National Academy Press, 1990), pp. 66-68.

6. Hayes, Palmer, and Zaslow, *Who Cares for America's Children?* pp. 70-71.

7. Hayes, Palmer, and Zaslow, *Who Cares for America's Children?* pp. 101-103.

8. Hayes, Palmer, and Zaslow, *Who Cares for America's Children?* pp. 84-86.

9. Hayes, Palmer, and Zaslow, *Who Cares for America's Children?* pp. 85-86, and Accreditation Guidelines of the National Association for the Education of Young Children.

10. Deborah A. Phillips, Sandra Scarr, and Kathleen McCartney, "Dimensions and Effects of Child Care Quality: The Bermuda Study," in *Quality in Child Care: What Does the Research Tell Us?* ed. Deborah A. Phillips, vol. 1 (Washington, D.C.: National Association for the Education of Young Children, 1987).

11. Hayes, Palmer, and Zaslow, *Who Cares for America's Children?* pp. 66-67.

12. Hayes, Palmer, and Zaslow, *Who Cares for America's Children?* pp. 66-67.

13. Hayes, Palmer, and Zaslow, *Who Cares for America's Children?* pp. 87-88.

14. Hayes, Palmer, and Zaslow, *Who Cares for America's Children?* p. 88.

15. Deborah A. Phillips, ed., *Quality in Child Care: What Does Research Tell Us?* vol. 1 (Washington, D.C.: National Association for the Education of Young Children, 1987), pp. 5-6.

16. Hayes, Palmer, and Zaslow, *Who Cares for America's Children?* pp. 89-90.

17. Hayes, Palmer, and Zaslow, *Who Cares for America's Children?* pp. 91-92.

18. Marcy Whitebook, Carollee Howes, and Deborah Phillips, *Who Cares?: Child Care Teachers and the Quality of Care in America*, Final Report of the National Child Care Staffing Study (Oakland, Calif.: Child Care Employee Project, 1990), p. 114.

19. Hayes, Palmer, and Zaslow, *Who Cares for America's Children?* p. 97.

20. National Association of State Boards of Education, National Task Force on School Readiness, *Caring Communities: Supporting Young Children and Families*, pp. 6, 19.

21. I. Lazar and R. Darlington, "Lasting Effects of Early Education: A Report of the Consortium for Longitudinal Studies," *Monographs of the Society for Research in Child Development* 47, no. 195 (1982).

22. W. Steven Barnett, "Benefits of Compensatory Preschool Education," *Journal of Human Resources*, 1990.

23. The Perry Preschool study was conducted by High Scope Educational Foundation in the mid-1960s. It followed the progress of a group of highly disadvantaged children from a one-year intensive preschool program to age nineteen and identified a number of important long-term social benefits for the program. At the end of the study, the children were more likely to have graduated and obtained employment and were less likely to have become pregnant as teenagers, to be on welfare, or to have repeated a grade or been placed in special education.

24. Barnett, "Benefits of Compensatory Preschool Education."

25. J. S. Fuerst and Dorothy Fuerst, "Chicago Experience with Early Childhood Program: The Special Case of the Child Parent Center Program," *Urban Education* 28, No. 1 (April 1993), and Dominic F. Gullo, *The Effects of Gender, At-Risk Status, and Number of Years in Preschool on Children's Academic Readiness* (Milwaukee: University of Wisconsin-Milwaukee, Department of Early Childhood Education, 1990).

26. Gullo, *The Effects of Gender, At-Risk Status, and Number of Years in Preschool on Children's Academic Readiness*.

27. Fuerst and Fuerst, "Chicago Experience with Early Childhood Program: The Special Case of the Child Parent Center Program."

28. Whitebook, Howes, and Phillips, *Who Cares?: Child Care Teachers and the Quality of Care in America*, pp. 70-75.

63

29. Whitebook, Howes, and Phillips. *Who Cares?: Child Care Teachers and the Quality of Care in America*, pp. 146-147.

30. Hayes, Palmer, and Zaslow, *Why Cares for America's Children?* p. 67.

31. Anne Mitchell, Emily Cooperstein, and Mary Larner, *Child Care Choices, Consumer Education, and Low-Income Families* (New York: National Center for Children in Poverty, Columbia University, 1992).

32. Kisker and Maynard, "Quality, Cost, and Parental Choice of Child Care," p. 130.

33. EDK Associates, *Choosing Quality Child Care*, A Qualitative Study Conducted in Houston, Hartford, West Palm Beach, Charlotte, Alameda, Los Angeles, Salem, and Minneapolis, Prepared by the Child Care Action Campaign, Sponsored by Dayton Hudson Foundation, January 1992.

34. EDK Associates, *Choosing Quality Child Care*.

35. EDK Associates, *Choosing Quality Child Care*.

36. Mitchell, Cooperstein, and Larner, *Child Care Choices, Consumer Education, and Low-Income Families*, p. 23.

37. Gina C. Adams, *Who Knows How Safe? The Status of State Efforts to Ensure Quality Child Care* (Washington, D.C.: Children's Defense Fund, September 1990), p. 1, and Linda J. Waite, Arleen Leibowitz, and Christina Witsberger, "What Parents Pay For: Child Care Characteristics, Quality, and Costs," *Journal of Social Issues* 47, no. 2 (1991): 33-48.

38. Kisker and Maynard, "Quality, Cost, and Parental Choice of Child Care," pp. 135-136, and Hayes, Palmer, and Zaslow, *Who Cares for America's Children?* pp. 241-242.

39. Hayes, Palmer, and Zaslow, *Who Cares for America's Children?* p. 72.

40. Whitebook, Howes, and Phillips, *Who Cares?: Child Care Teachers and the Quality of Care in America*, pp. 152-153.

41. Martha J. Zaslow, "Variation in Child Care Quality and Its Implications for Children," *Journal of Social Issues* 47, no. 2 (1991): 133.

42. Ellen Kisker et al., *A Profile of Child Care Settings: Early Education and Care in 1990*, vol. 1 (Washington, D.C.: U.S. Government Printing Office, 1991), p. 9.

43. Barbara Willer et al., *The Demand and Supply of Child Care in 1990* (Washington, D.C.: National Association for the Education of Young Children, 1991), pp. 25-29.

CHAPTER 3

1. Sandra L. Hofferth et al., *National Child Care Survey, 1990*, A National Association for the Education of Young Children Study (Washington, D.C.: The Urban Institute Press, 1991), pp. 120-122.

2. Ellen Galinsky and Dana Friedman, *Education Before School: Investing in Quality Child Care*, A Study Prepared for the Committee for Economic Development (New York: Scholastic Inc., 1993), p. 86.

3. Mary Culkin, John R. Morris, and Suzanne W. Helburn, "Quality and the True Cost of Child Care," *Journal of Social Issues* 47, no. 2 (1991): 83.

4. *Embracing Our Future: A Child Care Action Agenda* (Boston: The Boston Foundation, Carol R. Goldberg Seminar on Child Care, 1992), p. 54.

5. Barbara Willer et al., *The Demand and Supply of Child Care in 1990* (Washington, D.C.: National Association for the Education of Young Children, 1991), p. 48.

6. Sandra L. Hanson and Theodora Ooms, "The Economic Costs and Rewards of Two-Earner, Two-Parent Families," *Journal of Marriage and the Family* 53 (August 1991).

7. Hofferth et al., *National Child Care Survey, 1990*, pp. 176-178.

8. Hofferth et al., *National Child Care Survey, 1990*, p. 178.

9. William R. Prosser and Sharon M. McGroder, "The Supply of and Demand for Child Care: Measurement and Analytic Issues," in *Child Care in the 1990s: Trends and Consequences*, ed. Alan Booth (Hilldsdale, N.J.: Lawrence Erlbaum Associates, 1992), p. 45.

10. Prosser and McGroder, "The Supply of and Demand for Child Care: Measurement and Analytic Issues," p. 47.

11. Hofferth et al., *National Child Care Survey, 1990*, pp. 186-199.

12. Ellen Kisker et al., *A Profile of Child Care Settings: Early Education and Care in 1990* (Washington, D.C.: U.S. Government Printing Office, 1991), p. 9.

13. Prosser and McGroder, "The Supply of and Demand for Child Care: Measurement and Analytic Issues," p. 47.

14. Willer et al., *The Demand and Supply of Child Care in 1990*, p. 35.

15. Willer et al., *The Demand and Supply of Child Care in 1990*, p. 46

16. Willer et al., *The Demand and Supply of Child Care in 1990*, p. 41.

17. Victor R. Fuchs and Mary Coleman, "Small Children, Small Pay: Why Child Care Pays So Little," *The American Prospect* (Winter 1991): 70-79.

18. Galinsky and Friedman, *Education Before School*, Figure 4.6, p. 96.

19. Culkin, Morris, and Helburn, "Quality and the True Cost of Child Care," p. 7.

20. Philip K. Robins, "Federal Financing of Child Care: Alternative Approaches and Economic Implications" (Department of Economics, University of Miami, May 1988), p. 23.

21. Cheryl D. Hayes, John L. Palmer, and Martha J. Zaslow, eds., *Who Cares for America's Children?* (Washington, D.C.: Panel on Child Care Policy, National Research Council, National Academy Press, 1990), pp. 195-197.

22. Hayes, Palmer, and Zaslow, *Who Cares for America's Children?* p. 197

23. Hayes, Palmer, and Zaslow, *Who Cares for America's Children?* p. 197.

24. Sandra Hofferth, The Urban Institute, personal communication.

25. Hofferth et al., *National Child Care Survey, 1990*, p. 186.

26. Bruce Fuller et al., "Can Government Raise Child Care Quality?: The Influence of Family Demand, Poverty, and Policy," Initial Report to the Packard Foundation Center for the Future of the Child, September 1992.

27. Marcy Whitebook, Carollee Howes, and Deborah Phillips, *Who Cares?: Child Care Teachers and the Quality of Care in America*, Final Report of the National Child Care Staffing Study (Oakland, Calif.: Child Care Employee Project, 1990), pp. 145-151.

28. Fuller et al., "Can Government Raise Child Care Quality?: The Influence of Family Demand, Poverty, and Policy."

29. Sherrie Lookner, "Comparative Strengths of Vouchers & Contracts" (Washington, D.C.: Children's Defense Fund, draft, February 1992), pp. 1-3.

30. Sandra Hofferth, "How Do Parents Make Child Care Choices: Do Models of Parent Choice Bear Any Relevance to Reality?" (Paper delivered at the Ninth Annual Symposium, A.M. Mailman Family Foundation, Rye, N.Y., June 29, 1992).

31. Lookner, "Comparative Strengths of Vouchers & Contracts," pp. 2-3.

CHAPTER 4

1. Cheryl D. Hayes, John L. Palmer, and Martha J. Zaslow, *Who Cares for America's Children?* (Washington, D.C.: Panel on Child Care Policy, National Research Council, National Academy Press, 1990), p. 233.

2. Hayes, Palmer, and Zaslow, *Who Cares for America's Children?* p. 213.

3. Mark Greenberg, *Toward Seamless Service: Some Key Issues in the Relationship Between the Child Care and Development Block Grant and AFDC-Related Child Care* (Washington, D.C.: Center for Law and Social Policy, July 1991).

4. Children's Defense Fund, *Child Care Under the Family Support Act: Early Lessons from the States* (Washington, D.C.: Children's Defense Fund, 1992), p. xx, and Greenberg, *Toward Seamless Service: Some Key Issues in the Relationship Between the Child Care and Development Block Grant and AFDC-Related Child Care*.

5. Edward Zigler and Susan Muenchow, *Head Start: The Inside Story of America's Most Successful Educational Experiment* (New York: Basic Books, 1992), p. 229.

6. Zigler and Muenchow, *Head Start: The Inside Story of America's Most Successful Educational Experiment*, pp. 225-226.

7. Zigler and Muenchow, *Head Start: The Inside Story of America's Most Successful Educational Experiment*, p. 212, and Douglas J. Besharov, "Why Head Start Badly Needs a Restart," *The Washington Post National Weekly Edition*, February 10-16, 1992.

8. Zigler and Muenchow, *Head Start: The Inside Story of America's Most Successful Educational Experiment*, p. 225.

9. Zigler and Muenchow, *Head Start: The Inside Story of America's Most Successful Educational Experiment*, p. 214.

10. Zigler and Muenchow, *Head Start: The Inside Story of America's Most Successful Educational Experiment*, p. 221.

11. Sandra L. Hofferth, "The Demand for and Supply of Child Care in the 1990s," in *Child Care in the 1990s: Trends and Consequences*, ed. Alan Booth (Hillsdale, N.J.: Lawrence Erlbaum Associates, 1992), pp. 18-19.

13. Ellen Galinsky and Dana Friedman, *Education Before School: Investing in Quality Child Care*, A Study Prepared for the Committee for Economic Development (New York: Scholastic Inc., 1993), p. 47.

14. Galinsky and Friedman, *Education Before School: Investing in Quality Child Care*, p. 47.

15. Heidi I. Hartmann and Diana M. Pearce, *High Skill and Low Pay: The Economics of Child Care Work* (Washington, D.C.: Institute for Women's Policy Research, January 1989), p. 23.

16. Barbara Willer et. al., *The Demand and Supply of Child Care in 1990* (Washington, D.C.: National Association for the Education of Young Children, 1991), p. 16.

17. Hayes, Palmer, and Zaslow, *Who Cares for America's Children?* pp. 95-96.

18. Hayes, Palmer, and Zaslow, *Who Cares for America's Children?* pp. 95-96.

19. Gail Richardson and Elizabeth Marx, *A Welcome for Every Child: How France Achieves Quality in Child Care* (New York: The French-American Foundation, 1989).

20. Willer et al., *The Demand and Supply of Child Care in 1990*, p. 25.

21. Edward F. Zigler and Mary E. Lang, *Child Care Choices* (New York: The Free Press, 1991), pp. 78-80.

22. Jay Belsky, "A Reassessment of Infant Day Care," in *The Parental Leave Crisis: Toward a National Leave Policy*, ed. Edward F. Zigler and Meryl Frank (New Haven: Yale University Press, 1988), pp. 100-119.

23. Zigler and Lang, *Child Care Choices*, pp. 82-85.

24. Andrew Cherlin, "Infant Care and Full-Time Employment," in *Child Care in the 1990s: Trends and Consequences*, ed. Alan Booth (Hillsdale, N.J.: Lawrence Erlbaum Associates, 1992), p. 210.

25. Deborah Lowe Vandell and Janaki Ramanan, "Effects of Early and Recent Maternal Employment on Children from Low-Income Families," *Child Development* 63 (1992): 938-949.

26. Vandell and Ramanan, "Effects of Early and Recent Maternal Employment on Children from Low-Income Families," p. 947.

27. Ellen Kisker and Rebecca Maynard, "Quality, Cost, and Parental Choice of Child Care," in *The Economics of Child Care*, ed. David M. Blau (New York: Russell Sage Foundation, 1991), p. 133.

28. *Embracing Our Future: A Child Care Action Agenda* (Boston: The Boston Foundation, Carol R. Goldberg Seminar on Child Care, 1992), p. 54.

29. Karen Oppenheim Mason and Laura Duberstein, "Consequences of Child Care for Parents' Well-Being," in *Child Care in the 1990s: Trends and Consequences*, ed. Alan Booth (Hillsdale, N.J.: Lawrence Erlbaum Associates, 1992), p. 152.

30. Hayes, Palmer, and Zaslow, *Who Cares for America's Children?* p. 209

31. "Anticipating a Family Leave Law," *The New York Times*, January 31, 1993.

32. Hayes, Palmer, and Zaslow, *Who Cares for America's Children?* pp. 208-211.

33. Meryl Frank, "Cost, Financing, and Implementation Mechanisms of Parental Leave Policies," in *The Parental Leave Crisis: Toward a National Leave Policy*, ed. Edward F. Zigler and Meryl Frank (New Haven: Yale University Press, 1988), p. 317.

34. U.S. General Accounting Office, *Parental Leave: Revised Cost Estimate Reflecting the Impact of Spousal Leave* (Washington, D.C.: U.S. Government Printing Office, 1988).

35. Eileen Trzcinsky and William T. Alpert, "Job Guaranteed Medical Leave: Reducing Termination Costs to Business" (Paper presented at the 1992 World Congress on the Family, Columbus, Ohio, 1992).

36. Graham L. Staines and Ellen Galinsky, "Parental Leave and Productivity: The Supervisor's View," in *Parental Leave and Productivity*, ed. Dana E. Friedman, Ellen Galinsky, and Veronica Plowden (New York: Families and Work Institute, 1992).

37. Roberta M. Spalter-Roth and Heidi I. Hartmann, *Unnecessary Losses* (Washington, D.C.: Institute for Women's Policy Research, 1988).

38. Hayes, Palmer, and Zaslow, *Who Cares for America's Children?* p. 312.

39. Zigler and Lang, *Child Care Choices*, p. 198.

40. William T. Gormley, Jr., "State Regulations and the Availability of Child-Care Services," *Journal of Policy Analysis and Management* 10, no. 1: 78.

41. Ron Haskins, "Is Anything More Important than Day-Care Quality?" in *Child Care in the 1990s: Trends and Consequences*, ed. Alan Booth (Hillsdale, N.J.: Lawrence Erlbaum Associates, 1992), pp. 101-115.

42. Gormley, "State Regulations and the Availability of Child-Care Services," p. 90.

43. Hayes, Palmer, and Zaslow, *Who Cares for America's Children?* p. 310.

44. Carol Copple, "Quality Matters: Improving the Professional Development of the Early Childhood Work Force" (Report based on a meeting held at Carnegie Corporation of New York, November 7-9, 1990), p. 9.

45. Copple, "Quality Matters: Improving the Professional Development of the Early Childhood Work Force," pp. 8-9.

46. Gina C. Adams, *Who Knows How Safe?: The Status of State Efforts to Ensure Quality Child Care* (Washington, D.C.: Children's Defense Fund, September, 1990), pp. 1-2.

47. Adams, *Who Knows How Safe?: The Status of State Efforts to Ensure Quality Child Care*, pp. 3-4.

48. Gormley, "State Regulations and the Availability of Child-Care Services," pp. 90-91.

49. Rebecca Maynard and Eileen McGinnis, "Policies to Enhance Access to High-Quality Child Care," in *Child Care in the 1990s: Trends and Consequences*, ed. Alan Booth (Hillsdale, N.J.: Lawrence Earlbaum Associates, 1992), p. 205.

50. EDK Associates, *Choosing Quality Child Care*, A Qualitative Study Conducted in Houston, Hartford, West Palm Beach, Charlotte, Alameda, Los Angeles, Salem, and Minneapolis, Prepared by the Child Care Action Campaign, Sponsored by Dayton Hudson Foundation, January 1992.

51. Hayes, Palmer, and Zaslow, *Who Cares for America's Children?* p. 241.

52. Hayes, Palmer, and Zaslow, *Who Cares for America's Children?* pp. 221-222.

53. Hayes, Palmer, and Zaslow, *Who Cares for America's Children?* p. 173.

CHAPTER 5

1. Ellen Galinsky and Dana Friedman, *Education Before School: Investing in Quality Child Care*, A Study Prepared for the Committee for Economic Development (New York: Scholastic Inc., 1993), p. 123.

2. Sandra L. Hofferth et al., *National Child Care Survey, 1990*, A National Association for the Education of Young Children Study (Washington, D.C.: The Urban Institute Press, 1991), p. 358.

3. Hofferth et al., *National Child Care Survey, 1990*, p. 359.

4. Galinsky and Friedman, *Education Before School: Investing in Quality Child Care*, p. 132.

5. Ellen Galinsky, Dana E. Friedman, and Carol A. Hernandez, *The Corporate Reference Guide to Work-Family Programs* (New York: Families and Work Institute, 1991), pp. 212-213.

6. Galinsky, Friedman, and Hernandez, *The Corporate Reference Guide to Work-Family Programs*, pp. 214-216.

7. Galinsky, Friedman, and Hernandez, *The Corporate Reference Guide to Work-Family Programs*, pp. 216-217.

8. Child Care Action Campaign, *Not Too Small to Care: Small Businesses and Child Care* (New York: Child Care Action Campaign, September 1991), p. 17.

9. U.S. Department of Labor, Child Care Liability Insurance Task Force, *Employer Centers and Child Care Liability Insurance* (Washington, D.C.: U.S. Government Printing Office, December 1989).

10. Galinsky and Friedman, *Education Before School: Investing in Quality Child Care*, p. 133.

11. Galinsky, Friedman, and Hernandez, *The Corporate Reference Guide to Work-Family Programs*, pp. 239-240.

12. Galinsky, Friedman, and Hernandez, *The Corporate Reference Guide to Work-Family Programs*, pp. 253-257.

13. Galinsky, Friedman, and Hernandez, *The Corporate Reference Guide to Work-Family Programs*, pp. 260-263.

14. *Shareholders in the Future*, The Maryland Employers Advisory Council on Child Care, November 28, 1998.

15. Edward Zigler and Susan Muenchow, *Head Start: The Inside Story of America's Most Successful Educational Experiment* (New York: Basic Books, 1992).

16. *Shareholders in the Future*.

17. Galinsky and Friedman, *Education Before School: Investing in Quality Child Care*, p. 121.

18. Galinsky and Friedman, *Education Before School: Investing in Quality Child Care*, p. 121.

19. Deborah Stahl, AT&T, personal communication.

20. *Wall Street Journal*, October 17, 1991.

21. Dana E. Friedman and Margaret King, *Public-Private Partnerships for Child Care: A Feasibility Study for New York State* (New York: Families and Work Institute, 1992), pp. 22-23.

22. Friedman and King, *Public-Private Partnerships for Child Care: A Feasibility Study for New York State*, pp. 23-24.

MEMORANDA OF COMMENT, RESERVATION, OR DISSENT

Page 1, OWEN B. BUTLER, with which JAMES Q. RIORDAN has asked to be associated

I do not believe the policy statement gives sufficient weight to individual choices as opposed to "cultural, social, and economic changes " in explaining the increased demand for child care. Unmarried women do not become mothers entirely by accident — choices are made. Our society does not compel both parents of young children to enter the work force — choices are made. In many cases, parents of young children are not forced to separate — choices are made. Although the policy statement indicates on page 7 that living standards are reduced by the loss of unpaid household work when women go into the labor force, in my view, insufficient attention is paid to the parental investment in child rearing and other household duties, which are not counted in gross domestic product.

Pages 10 and 29, OWEN B. BUTLER, with which JAMES Q. RIORDAN has asked to be associated

While I agree we must invest more money in child care, I disagree vigorously with the proposal to make the dependent child care tax credit refundable. There is no evidence that simply mailing checks to parents who cannot (or choose not to) earn enough money to have any federal income tax liability is the most efficient and effective way to spend extra funds. As the policy statement repeatedly states, we must work on this problem with very limited resources. Each dollar we spend should be carefully and precisely targeted to programs that have been evaluated and have been proven to work.

The policy statement implies that the dependent care tax credit is misdirected because it favors "middle- and upper-income families." In fact this credit already makes our federal income tax much more "progressive." For example, a single parent earning about $15,000 per year and paying $2,400 for child care is able to exempt the equivalent of nearly twice that amount from taxable income (because the tax rate is only 15 percent while the credit is nearly 30 percent). On the other hand, a single parent earning substantially more than that amount is able to exempt the equivalent of only about two-thirds of the actual expenditure for child care (because the tax rate is about 30 percent and the credit is only 20 percent).

Page 48, LUCIO A. NOTO, with which JAMES Q. RIORDAN has asked to be associated

I am concerned that Chapter 5 of the policy statement does not address the cost aspects of corporate-provided child care programs. Corporate programs are highlighted without an indication as to how they may be related to the cost of other employee programs or a company's operations, geographical location, needs, preferences, and other considerations which drive decisions on child care or other choices on how to spend corporate money. Other chapters in the statement present a pragmatic view of child care issues with a comprehensive analysis of contributing factors. I would have like to have seen the same pragmatism and analysis applied to Chapter 5.

FUNDERS

Carnegie Corporation of New York

Champion International Corporation

Corning Incorporated

Dayton Hudson Foundation

E.I. Du Pont de Nemours & Company

The Ford Foundation

Johnson & Johnson Family of Companies

Kraft General Foods

The John D. & Catherine T. MacArthur Foundation

Primerica Foundation

The Stride Rite Foundation

OBJECTIVES OF THE COMMITTEE FOR ECONOMIC DEVELOPMENT

For 50 years, the Committee for Economic Development has been a respected influence on the formation of business and public policy. CED is devoted to these two objectives:

To develop, through objective research and informed discussion, findings and recommendations for private and public policy that will contribute to preserving and strengthening our free society, achieving steady economic growth at high employment and reasonably stable prices, increasing productivity and living standards, providing greater and more equal opportunity for every citizen, and improving the quality of life for all.

To bring about increasing understanding by present and future leaders in business, government, and education, and among concerned citizens, of the importance of these objectives and the ways in which they can be achieved.

CED's work is supported by private voluntary contributions from business and industry, foundations, and individuals. It is independent, nonprofit, nonpartisan, and nonpolitical.

Through this business-academic partnership, CED endeavors to develop policy statements and other research materials that commend themselves as guides to public and business policy; that can be used as texts in college economics and political science courses and in management training courses; that will be considered and discussed by newspaper and magazine editors, columnists, and commentators; and that are distributed abroad to promote better understanding of the American economic system.

CED believes that by enabling business leaders to demonstrate constructively their concern for the general welfare, it is helping business to earn and maintain the national and community respect essential to the successful functioning of the free enterprise capitalist system.

CED RESEARCH ADVISORY BOARD

CED PROFESSIONAL AND ADMINISTRATIVE STAFF

SOL HURWITZ
President

VAN DOORN OOMS
Senior Vice President and
  Director of Research

WILLIAM J. BEEMAN
Vice President and Director
  of Economic Studies

CLAUDIA P. FEUREY
Vice President and
  Director of Information

SANDRA KESSLER HAMBURG
Vice President and Director of
  Education Studies

TIMOTHY J. MUENCH
Vice President and Director of
  Finance and Administration

EVA POPPER
Vice President and Director of
  Development

NATHANIEL M. SEMPLE
Vice President, Secretary of
  the Research and Policy
  Committee, and Director,
  Business–Government Relations

Senior Economic Consultant
ROBERT C. HOLLAND

*Advisor on International
Economic Policy*
ISAIAH FRANK
William L. Clayton Professor
  of International Economics
The Johns Hopkins University

THOMAS L. MONAHAN, III
Director of Editorial Services

SHARON O'CONNELL
Director of Special Projects

THOMAS R. FLAHERTY
Comptroller

Research
MICHAEL K. BAKER
Policy Analyst

TERRA L. GEIGER
Policy Analyst

MICHAEL B. GREENSTONE
Policy Analyst

LORRAINE M. BROOKER
Research Administrator

Conferences
MARY ANN GENNUSA
Manager

Information and Publications
JULIE A. WON
Assistant Director

Development
JULIA R. HICKS
Assistant Director

ANA SOMOHANO
Campaign Coordinator

WILFORD V. MALCOLM
Campaign Production Administrator

Administration
DOROTHY M. STEFANSKI
Deputy Comptroller

ARLENE M. MURPHY
Administrative Assistant to
  the President

SHIRLEY R. SHERMAN
Office Manager, Washington

RONALD V. GUZMAN
Operations Manager

STATEMENTS ON NATIONAL POLICY ISSUED BY THE COMMITTEE FOR ECONOMIC DEVELOPMENT

SELECTED PUBLICATIONS:

What Price Clean Air? A Market Approach to Energy and Environmental Policy *(1993)*

Restoring Prosperity: Budget Choices for Economic Growth *(1992)*

The United States in the New Global Economy: A Rallier of Nations *(1992)*

The Economy and National Defense: Adjusting to Cutbacks in the Post-Cold War Era *(1991)*

Politics, Tax Cuts and the Peace Dividend *(1991)*

The Unfinished Agenda: A New Vision for Child Development and Education *(1991)*

Foreign Investment in the United States: What Does It Signal? *(1990)*

An America That Works: The Life-Cycle Approach to a Competitive Work Force *(1990)*

Breaking New Ground in U.S. Trade Policy *(1990)*

Battling America's Budget Deficits *(1989)*

*Strengthening U.S.-Japan Economic Relations *(1989)*

Who Should Be Liable? A Guide to Policy for Dealing with Risk *(1989)*

Investing in America's Future: Challenges and Opportunities for Public Sector Economic Policies *(1988)*

Children in Need: Investment Strategies for the Educationally Disadvantaged *(1987)*

Finance and Third World Economic Growth *(1987)*

Toll of the Twin Deficits *(1987)*

Reforming Health Care: A Market Prescription *(1987)*

Work and Change: Labor Market Adjustment Policies in a Competitive World *(1987)*

Leadership for Dynamic State Economies *(1986)*

Investing in Our Children: Business and the Public Schools *(1985)*

Fighting Federal Deficits: The Time for Hard Choices *(1985)*

Strategy for U.S. Industrial Competitiveness *(1984)*

Strengthening the Federal Budget Process: A Requirement for Effective Fiscal Control *(1983)*

Productivity Policy: Key to the Nation's Economic Future *(1983)*

Energy Prices and Public Policy *(1982)*

Public-Private Partnership: An Opportunity for Urban Communities *(1982)*

Reforming Retirement Policies *(1981)*

Transnational Corporations and Developing Countries: New Policies for a Changing World Economy *(1981)*

Fighting Inflation and Rebuilding a Sound Economy *(1980)*

Stimulating Technological Progress *(1980)*

Helping Insure Our Energy Future: A Program for Developing Synthetic Fuel Redefining
  Government's Role in the Market System *(1979)*

Improving Management of the Public Work Force: The Challenge to State and Local Government *(1978)*

Jobs for the Hard-to-Employ: New Directions for a Public-Private Partnership *(1978)*

An Approach to Federal Urban Policy *(1977)*

Key Elements of a National Energy Strategy *(1977)*

Nuclear Energy and National Security *(1976)*

Fighting Inflation and Promoting Growth *(1976)*

Improving Productivity in State and Local Government *(1976)*

*International Economic Consequences of High-Priced Energy *(1975)*

Broadcasting and Cable Television: Policies for Diversity and Change *(1975)*

Achieving Energy Independence *(1974)*

A New U.S. Farm Policy for Changing World Food Needs *(1974)*

Congressional Decision Making for National Security *(1974)*

*Toward a New International Economic System: A Joint Japanese-American View *(1974)*

More Effective Programs for a Cleaner Environment *(1974)*

The Management and Financing of Colleges *(1973)*

Financing the Nation's Housing Needs *(1973)*

Building a National Health-Care System *(1973)*

High Employment Without Inflation: A Positive Program for Economic Stabilization *(1972)*

Reducing Crime and Assuring Justice *(1972)*

Military Manpower and National Security *(1972)*

The United States and the European Community: Policies for a Changing World Economy *(1971)*

Social Responsibilities of Business Corporations *(1971)*

*Statements issued in association with CED counterpart organizations in foreign countries.

CED COUNTERPART ORGANIZATIONS

Close relations exist between the Committee for Economic Development and independent, nonpolitical research organizations in other countries. Such counterpart groups are composed of business executives and scholars and have objectives similar to those of CED, which they pursue by similarly objective methods. CED cooperates with these organizations on research and study projects of common interest to the various countries concerned. This program has resulted in a number of joint policy statements involving such international matters as energy, East-West trade, assistance to developing countries, and the reduction of nontariff barriers to trade.

CE	Circulo de Empresarios Madrid, Spain
CEDA	Committee for Economic Development of Australia Sydney, Australia
CEPES	Vereinigung für Wirtschaftlichen Fortschritt E.V. Frankfurt, Germany
FORUM	Forum de Administradores de Empresas Lisbon, Portugal
IE	Institut de L'Entreprise Brussels, Belgium
IE	Institut de l'Entreprise Paris, France
IEA	Institute of Economic Affairs London, England
IW	Institut der Deutschen Wirtschaft Cologne, Germany
経済同友会	Keizai Doyukai Tokyo, Japan
SNS	Studieförbundet Naringsliv och Samhälle Stockholm, Sweden